Understanding Migration Economics

Understanding Migration Economy

Government And the Economy, Volume 1

Sixolisiwe Dabula

Published by Sixolisiwe Dabula, 2024.

While every precaution has been taken in the preparation of this book, the publisher assumes no responsibility for errors or omissions, or for damages resulting from the use of the information contained herein.

UNDERSTANDING MIGRATION ECONOMY

First edition. August 3, 2024.

ISBN: 979-8227562302

Written by Sixolisiwe Dabula.

Table of Contents

To the Readers

Thank you for your support

Urban Shifts: Gentrification and the Rural Exodus

Introduction

Overview of Gentrification and Rural-to-Urban Migration

Gentrification and rural-to-urban migration are two of the most significant and intertwined social phenomena shaping the modern world. They represent complex and multifaceted processes that have profound implications for individuals, communities, and entire societies. Understanding these dynamics is crucial for grasping the current and future landscapes of urban and rural areas alike.

Gentrification is a term that has gained widespread usage in recent decades, often evoking strong emotions and debates among policymakers, urban planners, and residents alike. At its core, gentrification refers to the process by which urban neighbourhoods, typically those that have been economically depressed or marginalised, experience an influx of wealthier residents. This influx leads to rising property values, changes in the neighbourhood's character, and often, the displacement of long-standing, lower-income residents. While gentrification can bring economic revitalization and new amenities to previously neglected areas, it also raises critical questions about social equity, cultural preservation, and the right to the city.

Rural-to-urban migration, on the other hand, is a demographic shift that has been occurring for centuries but has accelerated dramatically in the last century. This movement involves people leaving rural areas, often driven by a lack of economic opportunities, in search of better prospects in urban centres. This migration is not just a local or national phenomenon but a global one, with significant impacts on both the rural areas left behind and the urban areas that receive these migrants.

The interplay between gentrification and rural-to-urban migration is a central theme of this book. As people move from rural to urban areas, they contribute to the growth and transformation of cities. In some cases, this influx can spur gentrification, as new populations with different economic resources and cultural preferences settle in urban neighbourhoods. Conversely, the effects of gentrification can influence patterns of migration, as displaced urban residents may seek new homes in less developed or more affordable areas, potentially even reversing the flow to rural areas in certain contexts.

This book aims to explore these processes in depth, examining their causes, consequences, and the broader social, economic, and cultural impacts they have. We will delve into the historical context that has shaped contemporary patterns of gentrification and migration, analyse the driving forces behind these trends, and consider the implications for future urban and rural development.

The rise of global cities, the decline of rural economies, and the transformation of urban neighbourhoods are all part of a broader narrative of change that this book seeks to unravel. Through a combination of theoretical insights, case studies, and empirical research, we will explore how gentrification and rural-to-urban migration are reshaping the world we live in, with a particular focus on the challenges and opportunities they present for creating more equitable, sustainable, and inclusive communities.

As we embark on this exploration, it is essential to recognize that gentrification and rural-to-urban migration are not isolated phenomena. They are deeply interconnected with other social, economic, and political processes, including globalisation, economic restructuring, and changes in housing policies. By situating these processes within a broader context, this book will provide a comprehensive understanding of the forces driving urban and rural transformation in the 21st century.

Chapter 2: Historical Context

Urbanization Trends Through the Ages

Urbanisation, the process by which rural populations move into cities, leading to the growth and development of urban areas, has been a defining feature of human civilization. From the ancient cities of Mesopotamia and the Indus Valley to the sprawling metropolises of the 21st century, urbanisation has shaped the economic, social, and cultural evolution of societies.

In ancient times, cities emerged as centres of trade, religion, and governance. The first urban settlements, such as Uruk in Mesopotamia, Mohenjo-Daro in the Indus Valley, and ancient Egyptian cities along the Nile, were hubs of early civilization. These cities were relatively small compared to modern standards but played crucial roles in the development of writing, trade networks, and centralised governments. Urbanisation during this period was slow and limited to specific regions, with the majority of the global population living in rural areas.

The Middle Ages saw the growth of cities as centres of commerce and craftsmanship, particularly in Europe and Asia. The rise of trade routes, such as the Silk Road, facilitated the exchange of goods and ideas, leading to the growth of cities like Constantinople, Baghdad, and Venice. These cities became melting pots of cultures and were crucial in the development of early banking, trade guilds, and educational institutions. Despite this growth, urbanisation was still limited, with most people engaged in agriculture and living in rural communities.

The Renaissance and the Age of Exploration in the 15th and 16th centuries marked a turning point in urbanisation. The expansion of European empires, the rise of mercantilism, and the discovery of new trade routes led to the growth of port cities like Lisbon, Amsterdam, and London. These cities became global centres of trade, finance, and culture, attracting migrants from rural areas and other parts of the world. Urbanisation began to accelerate, laying the groundwork for the significant demographic shifts that would occur in the following centuries.

The Industrial Revolution and Urban Migration

The Industrial Revolution, which began in the late 18th century in Britain and spread to other parts of Europe and North America, was a transformative period in human history. It marked the transition from agrarian economies to industrialised and urbanised societies. The revolution was driven by technological innovations, such as the steam engine, mechanised looms, and the development of the factory system.

As industries grew, so did the demand for labour. Rural populations, who had traditionally relied on agriculture for their livelihoods, began to migrate to urban areas in search of work. This migration was driven by the promise of higher wages, better living conditions, and the opportunity to escape the uncertainties of agricultural life. Cities like Manchester, Birmingham, and Liverpool in England saw explosive growth, transforming from small towns to industrial powerhouses within a few decades.

However, this rapid urbanisation came at a cost. The influx of people into cities outpaced the development of infrastructure, leading to overcrowded and unsanitary living conditions. The working class lived in cramped, poorly constructed housing, often in close proximity to factories that belched smoke and pollution into the air. Diseases such as cholera and tuberculosis were rampant, and life expectancy for urban workers was significantly lower than that of their rural counterparts.

Despite these challenges, the Industrial Revolution laid the foundation for modern urbanisation. The development of transportation networks, such as railways and steamships, facilitated the movement of goods and people, further accelerating the growth of cities. Urban centres became the epicentres of economic activity, innovation, and cultural exchange, attracting even more migrants from rural areas and contributing to the global trend of urbanisation.

Post-War Suburbanization and the Decline of Inner Cities

The aftermath of World War II brought about significant changes in urbanisation patterns, particularly in the Western world. The war had devastated many European cities, leading to massive reconstruction efforts. At the same time, economic growth in the United States fueled a new trend: suburbanization.

Suburbanization refers to the movement of people from urban centres to the surrounding suburbs, facilitated by the expansion of road networks, the availability of affordable housing, and the rise of the automobile. In the U.S., government policies, such as the GI Bill, provided returning soldiers with low-interest home loans, spurring a housing boom in the suburbs. This period saw the emergence of the "American Dream" ideal, characterised by homeownership, car ownership, and a lifestyle centred around suburban living.

While suburbanization offered many families a higher quality of life, it also had profound effects on inner cities. As middle-class families moved to the suburbs, urban centres experienced a decline in population and economic activity. Many inner-city neighbourhoods, particularly those inhabited by lower-income and minority populations, faced disinvestment, leading to deteriorating infrastructure, high crime rates, and declining property values.

This decline was exacerbated by the phenomenon of "white flight," where white residents left urban areas in large numbers, leaving behind predominantly minority communities that were often marginalised and neglected by public policy. The result was a deepening of racial and economic segregation, with wealthier, predominantly white populations residing in the suburbs and poorer, predominantly minority populations remaining in the urban core.

The decline of inner cities in the post-war period set the stage for the gentrification processes that would begin in the latter half of the 20th century. As cities sought to revitalise their downtown areas and attract new investment, they implemented policies aimed at encouraging redevelopment, often leading to the displacement of long-time residents and the transformation of urban neighbourhoods.

In summary, urbanisation has been a continuous process throughout history, shaped by technological, economic, and social changes. The Industrial Revolution marked a significant acceleration of this process, leading to the growth of cities and the migration of rural populations to urban areas. The post-war era introduced the phenomenon of suburbanization, which altered the dynamics of urbanisation and set the stage for the gentrification trends that continue to shape cities today. As we explore these dynamics further in this book, we will see how the historical context of urbanisation and migration continues to influence contemporary patterns of gentrification and rural-to-urban migration.

Chapter 3: Understanding Gentrification

Definition and Characteristics of Gentrification

Gentrification is a complex and multifaceted process that involves the transformation of urban neighbourhoods, often leading to significant economic, social, and cultural changes. At its core, gentrification refers to the process by which lower-income, historically marginalised neighbourhoods experience an influx of wealthier residents, businesses, and investments, resulting in increased property values, shifts in the local demographic composition, and changes in the neighbourhood's character and culture.

While the term "gentrification" was first coined by British sociologist Ruth Glass in 1964 to describe the influx of middle-class residents into working-class neighbourhoods in London, the phenomenon has since become a global issue, affecting cities across the world. Gentrification is characterised by several key features:

1. **Economic Displacement**: One of the most prominent characteristics of gentrification is the economic displacement of long-standing residents and businesses. As property values and rents rise, many lower-income residents and small businesses are priced out of the neighbourhood, forced to relocate to more affordable areas. This displacement often disproportionately affects minority and working-class communities.

2. **Demographic Shifts**: Gentrification often leads to significant changes in the demographic composition of a neighbourhood. As wealthier individuals and families move in, the neighbourhood's socioeconomic status changes, often resulting in a decline in the proportion of lower-income and

minority residents. This shift can lead to the erosion of the neighbourhood's historical identity and culture.

3. **Cultural Transformation**: The influx of new residents and businesses often brings about a cultural transformation in the neighbourhood. Traditional shops, restaurants, and community centres may be replaced by upscale boutiques, cafes, and art galleries catering to the tastes and preferences of the new, wealthier residents. This cultural shift can lead to tensions between long-standing residents and newcomers, as well as a loss of the neighbourhood's unique character.

4. **Urban Redevelopment**: Gentrification is often accompanied by significant urban redevelopment efforts. This can include the renovation of old buildings, the construction of new housing developments, and the improvement of public spaces and infrastructure. While these changes can enhance the neighbourhood's physical environment, they can also contribute to the displacement of lower-income residents who can no longer afford to live in the area.

5. **Increased Economic Activity**: As gentrification takes hold, neighbourhoods often experience an increase in economic activity. New businesses, such as restaurants, shops, and entertainment venues, open to cater to the new residents, leading to job creation and increased tax revenues for the city. However, this economic growth can also exacerbate inequality if the benefits are not shared equitably among all residents.

The Process of Gentrification: Stages and Phases

Gentrification is not a sudden or uniform process; it typically unfolds in distinct stages or phases, each characterised by specific dynamics and changes within the neighbourhood. Understanding these stages can help identify the patterns and potential outcomes of gentrification in different contexts.

1. **Pioneer Stage**:

   ○ In the early stages of gentrification, artists, bohemians, and other creative individuals, often seeking affordable housing and studio space, move into economically depressed or neglected urban neighbourhoods. These pioneers are typically attracted by the lower cost of living, the availability of large, adaptable spaces, and the neighbourhood's potential for creative expression.

   ○ During this stage, the neighbourhood begins to develop a reputation as an "up-and-coming" or "edgy" area, attracting a small but growing number of new residents and businesses that share similar values and aesthetics.

2. **Early Gentrification Stage**:

   ○ As word spreads about the neighbourhood's potential and unique cultural scene, a second wave of gentrifiers—often young professionals and middle-class families—begins to move in. These new residents are attracted by the neighbourhood's creative vibe, proximity to urban amenities, and relatively affordable housing options compared to more established areas.

   ○ At this stage, property developers and investors start to take notice, leading to the renovation of older buildings, the construction of new housing, and the opening of new businesses catering to the tastes of the incoming residents.

Property values and rents begin to rise, and the neighbourhood's character starts to change more visibly.

3. Mid-Gentrification Stage:

○ As the neighbourhood becomes more desirable, the pace of change accelerates. More affluent individuals and families move in, driving up property values and rents even further. The influx of capital leads to the rapid development of new amenities, such as restaurants, cafes, boutiques, and art galleries, often at the expense of long-standing local businesses.

○ The demographic shifts become more pronounced, with lower-income residents increasingly being displaced due to rising costs. The cultural and social fabric of the neighbourhood begins to erode as the original community is replaced by new, wealthier residents.

4. Late Gentrification Stage:

○ In the final stage of gentrification, the neighbourhood has fully transitioned into a high-cost, high-status area. Property values and rents have reached levels comparable to or even exceeding those of more established, affluent neighbourhoods.

○ The original working-class or lower-income community has largely been displaced, and the neighbourhood's cultural identity has been transformed to align with the tastes and preferences of the new, wealthier residents. The area may now be marketed as a desirable destination for shopping, dining, and entertainment, attracting both locals and tourists.

○ This stage often brings increased scrutiny and criticism, as the negative consequences of gentrification—such as displacement, inequality, and cultural homogenization—become more apparent. In some cases, efforts to mitigate these impacts, such as affordable housing initiatives or community preservation projects, may be implemented, although these measures often struggle to reverse the broader trends.

Drivers of Gentrification: Economic, Social, and Cultural Factors

The process of gentrification is driven by a complex interplay of economic, social, and cultural factors. Understanding these drivers is essential for analysing why and how gentrification occurs, as well as for developing strategies to manage its impacts.

1. **Economic Drivers**:

○ **Real Estate Investment**: One of the primary economic drivers of gentrification is the investment in real estate by developers, investors, and property owners. As urban land becomes more valuable, there is a strong financial incentive to purchase and develop properties in lower-cost neighbourhoods that are perceived to have growth potential. This investment leads to rising property values and rents, driving the gentrification process.

○ **Urban Redevelopment Policies**: Government policies and incentives, such as tax breaks, zoning changes, and public infrastructure improvements, can also drive gentrification. These policies are often aimed at revitalising economically depressed areas but can lead to the displacement of existing residents if not carefully managed.

○ **Economic Restructuring**: The shift from industrial to service-based economies in many cities has also contributed to gentrification. As traditional manufacturing jobs decline, cities have sought to attract knowledge-based industries, such as finance, technology, and creative industries, leading to the transformation of urban neighbourhoods and the influx of higher-income residents.

2. Social Drivers:

○ **Demographic Changes**: Changes in population demographics, such as the ageing of the baby boomer generation, the rise of dual-income households, and the increasing number of young professionals seeking urban living, have contributed to the demand for housing in cities. These demographic shifts have driven gentrification in many urban areas, as new residents seek out neighbourhoods that offer convenience, amenities, and a sense of community.

○ **Education and Mobility**: Higher levels of education and increased social mobility among younger generations have also played a role in driving gentrification. Educated and upwardly mobile individuals are more likely to seek out urban living, contributing to the demand for housing in gentrifying neighbourhoods.

3. Cultural Drivers:

○ **Cultural Capital**: The desire for cultural capital—the social assets that promote social mobility, such as education, intellect, style, and taste—has become a significant driver of gentrification. Many gentrifiers are drawn to neighbourhoods that offer a sense of authenticity, creativity, and diversity, often associated with working-class or minority communities. This cultural appeal can drive the influx of new residents and the transformation of the neighbourhood's character.

○ **Lifestyle Preferences**: Changing lifestyle preferences, particularly among younger generations, have also contributed to gentrification. The desire for walkable neighbourhoods, access to cultural amenities, and proximity to work and social activities has led many individuals to choose urban living over suburban or rural lifestyles. This trend has driven the demand for housing in gentrifying neighbourhoods.

In conclusion, gentrification is a complex process driven by a combination of economic, social, and cultural factors. It unfolds in distinct stages, each characterised by specific changes in the neighbourhood's demographic, economic, and cultural landscape. Understanding these dynamics is essential for analysing the impacts of gentrification and for developing strategies to manage its effects on urban communities. As we continue to explore the themes of this book, we will delve deeper into the implications of gentrification and rural-to-urban migration for cities and rural areas alike.

Chapter 4: Rural-to-Urban Migration

Causes of Rural Exodus: Economic Disparities, Lack of Opportunities, and Agricultural Decline

Rural-to-urban migration, often referred to as the "rural exodus," is a phenomenon where large numbers of people leave rural areas in search of better opportunities in urban centres. This migration is driven by a variety of factors, primarily economic disparities, lack of opportunities in rural regions, and the decline of traditional agricultural practices.

1. **Economic Disparities**:

○ The most significant driver of rural-to-urban migration is the stark economic disparity between rural and urban areas. In many countries, urban centres offer more diverse and better-paying job opportunities compared to rural regions, where employment is often limited to agriculture or low-wage, unskilled labour. This economic gap encourages people, particularly the younger generation, to move to cities in search of better livelihoods.

○ Industrialization and globalisation have further widened this gap. Urban areas have become hubs for industries, services, and technology-driven economies, offering higher wages, better working conditions, and opportunities for career advancement. Conversely, rural areas, which often rely on agriculture and small-scale industries, struggle to compete in a globalised economy, leading to declining incomes and job opportunities.

2. **Lack of Opportunities**:

○ Beyond economic factors, rural areas often suffer from a lack of educational, healthcare, and social opportunities, which drives people to migrate to urban areas. Access to quality education and healthcare is typically more limited in rural regions, forcing residents to move to cities where these services are more readily available and of higher quality.

○ Additionally, rural areas often lack infrastructure and amenities that are taken for granted in urban centres, such as reliable transportation, communication networks, and entertainment options. This lack of opportunities for personal and professional growth makes urban areas more attractive, particularly to younger generations seeking a better quality of life.

3. **Agricultural Decline**:

○ The decline of agriculture as a viable livelihood has also contributed to the rural exodus. In many parts of the world, traditional farming practices have become less sustainable due to factors such as climate change, soil degradation, water scarcity, and market volatility. Smallholder farmers, in particular, struggle to make a living, leading to a decrease in the viability of agriculture as a primary source of income.

○ Moreover, the mechanisation and industrialization of agriculture have reduced the demand for labour in rural areas. Large-scale farming operations and the use of advanced technologies have made traditional farming practices less labour-intensive, leading to job losses and pushing rural workers to seek employment in urban areas.

Patterns of Migration: Domestic and

International Perspectives

Rural-to-urban migration is a global phenomenon, but the patterns of migration vary depending on the country, region, and specific socioeconomic conditions. These patterns can be observed at both domestic and international levels, each with its own unique dynamics and implications.

1. **Domestic Migration**:

○ Within countries, rural-to-urban migration often follows predictable patterns. People typically move from rural areas to nearby small or medium-sized cities before eventually migrating to larger metropolitan areas. This stepwise migration allows individuals to gradually adapt to urban life, find better employment opportunities, and build networks in urban centres.

○ In developing countries, rural-to-urban migration has been particularly pronounced, leading to the rapid growth of megacities. For example, in countries like China, India, and Brazil, millions of people have migrated from rural areas to cities in search of better opportunities, contributing to the explosive growth of urban populations.

○ The pattern of domestic migration is also influenced by regional disparities within countries. In countries like the United States and Mexico, for instance, migration is often directed towards economically prosperous regions or cities with thriving industries, such as Silicon Valley, New York, or Mexico City.

2. **International Migration**:

○ In addition to domestic migration, rural populations often migrate internationally in search of better opportunities. This is particularly common in countries where economic conditions, political instability, or environmental degradation make it difficult to sustain a livelihood in rural areas.

○ International migration from rural areas is often driven by the same factors as domestic migration, such as economic disparities and lack of opportunities. However, international migrants may also seek to escape conflict, political persecution, or environmental disasters, making migration a matter of survival rather than just economic betterment.

○ Remittances from international migrants play a crucial role in supporting rural communities left behind. These financial transfers help improve living conditions, fund education, and healthcare, and provide capital for small businesses, thereby mitigating some of the negative impacts of rural-to-urban migration.

Impacts on Rural Communities: Depopulation, Aging Population, and Economic Decline

Rural-to-urban migration has profound and often negative impacts on the communities left behind. As people leave rural areas in search of better opportunities, these regions face challenges such as depopulation, an ageing population, and economic decline, which can have long-lasting consequences for the social and economic fabric of rural life.

1. Depopulation:

○ One of the most visible impacts of rural-to-urban migration is depopulation. As younger and more mobile residents leave for urban areas, rural communities experience a significant decrease in population. This depopulation can lead to the closure of schools, healthcare facilities, and businesses, further eroding the viability of rural areas as places to live and work.

○ Depopulation also results in the loss of social cohesion and community spirit. In many rural areas, the departure of residents disrupts traditional social networks and weakens the bonds that hold communities together. This can lead to a sense of isolation among those who remain and a decline in communal activities and cultural practices.

2. Ageing Population:

○ As younger people migrate to urban areas, rural communities are left with an ageing population. This demographic shift poses significant challenges, as older residents may require more healthcare and social services, while there are fewer young people to provide care or contribute to the local economy.

○ The ageing population in rural areas can also lead to labour shortages, particularly in agriculture and other traditional industries that rely on manual labour. This can further weaken the economic base of rural communities and accelerate the decline of local economies.

3. Economic Decline:

○ The combined effects of depopulation and an aging population often lead to economic decline in rural areas.

As the working-age population dwindles, local businesses struggle to find employees, leading to closures and a reduction in economic activity. The decline in population also reduces demand for goods and services, further shrinking the local economy.

○ Additionally, the loss of young, educated individuals, often referred to as "brain drain," deprives rural areas of the human capital needed to drive innovation and economic development. This makes it challenging for rural communities to attract investment or develop new industries, perpetuating the cycle of economic decline.

○ In some cases, rural communities may become entirely abandoned, turning into "ghost towns" as the last residents move away or pass on. These abandoned areas represent the most extreme outcome of rural-to-urban migration, where the economic and social fabric of the community has completely unravelled.

In summary, rural-to-urban migration is a powerful force that reshapes both the urban and rural landscapes. While it offers opportunities for individuals to improve their lives and contributes to the growth of cities, it also poses significant challenges for rural communities, leading to depopulation, an ageing population, and economic decline. Understanding these dynamics is crucial for developing policies and strategies that can mitigate the negative impacts of rural-to-urban migration and promote more balanced and sustainable development across regions.

Chapter 5: Urban Resurgence: The Attraction of Cities

Economic Opportunities and Employment in Urban Centers

Urban centres have long been magnets for people seeking economic opportunities and employment, a trend that has only intensified in recent decades. Cities offer a diverse range of job opportunities that are often unavailable in rural areas, driving migration and fueling urban growth. The concentration of industries, businesses, and services in cities creates a dynamic labour market that attracts individuals from various socioeconomic backgrounds.

1. **Diverse Employment Opportunities**:

   ○ Cities are hubs of economic activity, housing a wide variety of industries, from manufacturing and technology to finance, retail, and hospitality. This diversity provides job seekers with a broad spectrum of employment options, catering to different skills, education levels, and career aspirations. Whether one is looking for entry-level positions, specialised roles, or entrepreneurial ventures, urban centres offer numerous opportunities for career advancement and economic mobility.

   ○ The rise of the knowledge economy, characterised by industries that rely on intellectual capabilities rather than physical inputs, has further boosted urban employment opportunities. Sectors such as information technology, finance, media, and professional services are predominantly urban-based, drawing highly skilled workers to cities in search of lucrative and prestigious jobs.

2. Higher Wages and Better Working Conditions:

○ Urban areas typically offer higher wages compared to rural regions. The concentration of businesses and competition for talent in cities drives up wages, making urban employment more attractive. Additionally, cities often have better labour protections, unions, and regulations that ensure safer working conditions and greater job security for workers.

○ The availability of diverse industries and employers in cities also allows workers to negotiate better terms, switch jobs more easily, and pursue career paths that align with their long-term goals. This fluidity and flexibility in the urban labour market stand in contrast to the limited opportunities and often stagnant economic conditions in rural areas.

3. Access to Markets and Resources:

○ For entrepreneurs and business owners, cities provide access to larger markets, a wider customer base, and essential resources such as capital, infrastructure, and skilled labour. The concentration of consumers and businesses in urban areas creates a fertile environment for startups and small businesses to thrive.

○ Cities also offer better access to financial institutions, investment opportunities, and government support programs, which can be crucial for business growth and sustainability. The proximity to suppliers, distributors, and clients in urban centres further enhances the efficiency and profitability of businesses, making cities attractive destinations for economic activity.

The Role of Education and Healthcare in Urban Migration

Education and healthcare are critical factors that influence people's decisions to migrate from rural areas to urban centres. Cities are often seen as centres of excellence in these sectors, offering better access, quality, and variety than what is typically available in rural regions.

1. **Access to Quality Education**:

○ Urban centres are home to a concentration of educational institutions, ranging from primary and secondary schools to prestigious universities and vocational training centres. These institutions offer higher-quality education, diverse curricula, and specialised programs that are often lacking in rural areas.

○ The availability of advanced education and research facilities in cities attracts students and families seeking better educational opportunities and future career prospects. Access to well-equipped schools, experienced teachers, and extracurricular activities in urban areas enhances students' learning experiences and outcomes, making cities attractive destinations for those prioritising education.

○ Higher education institutions in cities also play a crucial role in attracting and retaining talent. Universities and colleges often collaborate with industries, offering internships, research opportunities, and job placements that connect students with the urban labour market. This synergy between education and employment strengthens the appeal of cities as centres of learning and professional development.

2. Advanced Healthcare Services:

○ Cities are often at the forefront of healthcare innovation, offering advanced medical services, specialised treatments, and cutting-edge technology that are not available in rural areas. Urban centres typically have well-established healthcare infrastructures, including hospitals, clinics, and specialised medical facilities that provide a wide range of services.

○ Access to specialised healthcare professionals, such as surgeons, specialists, and mental health providers, is another significant draw for urban migration. The concentration of healthcare resources in cities ensures that residents have access to comprehensive care, including preventive services, emergency care, and chronic disease management.

○ For individuals with specific health needs or those seeking better healthcare for their families, the availability of quality healthcare in cities is a powerful motivator for migration. The promise of better health outcomes, longevity, and well-being drives many to leave rural areas in favour of urban living.

3. Educational and Healthcare Inequalities:

○ The disparities between urban and rural areas in terms of education and healthcare access contribute to the ongoing rural-to-urban migration. In many rural regions, schools are underfunded, lack qualified teachers, and have limited resources, leading to poorer educational outcomes and fewer opportunities for students. Similarly, rural healthcare facilities are often understaffed, under-resourced, and distant, making it difficult for residents to receive timely and adequate care.

○ These inequalities create a push factor, where rural residents, particularly young people and families, feel compelled to move to cities to access the quality education and healthcare necessary for a better life. This migration not only affects the individuals and families involved but also contributes to the broader depopulation and decline of rural areas.

Cultural and Social Pull: The Appeal of City Life

Beyond economic and practical considerations, cities hold a powerful cultural and social appeal that draws people from rural areas and smaller towns. The vibrancy, diversity, and opportunities for personal and social fulfilment in urban environments make cities attractive places to live.

1. **Cultural Diversity and Experiences**:

○ Cities are melting pots of cultures, ideas, and lifestyles. The diversity of urban populations brings together people from different backgrounds, ethnicities, and walks of life, creating a rich tapestry of cultural experiences. This diversity is reflected in the wide range of cultural institutions, such as museums, theatres, galleries, and music venues, which offer residents and visitors endless opportunities for exploration and enjoyment.

○ The cultural vibrancy of cities extends to the culinary scene, festivals, and community events, where people can experience different cuisines, traditions, and art forms from around the world. This constant exposure to new ideas and experiences is a significant draw for those seeking a dynamic and stimulating environment.

2. Social Connectivity and Networking:

○ Urban centres are hubs of social activity, offering numerous opportunities for networking, making friends, and building professional and personal relationships. The concentration of people in cities creates a lively social scene, with various events, meetups, and clubs catering to different interests and communities.

○ For young professionals, artists, and entrepreneurs, cities provide a fertile ground for collaboration and innovation. The ability to connect with like-minded individuals, access mentorship and resources, and participate in vibrant social and professional networks is a significant advantage of urban living.

○ Cities also offer greater anonymity and social freedom, allowing individuals to explore their identities and lifestyles in ways that might be more constrained in rural areas. The acceptance of diversity and the availability of niche communities make urban environments appealing to those seeking personal growth and social fulfilment.

3. Access to Amenities and Entertainment:

○ The convenience and variety of amenities in cities are major factors in their appeal. Urban residents enjoy easy access to shopping centres, restaurants, gyms, parks, and entertainment venues, all of which contribute to a high quality of life. The availability of public transportation, modern infrastructure, and technological advancements further enhances the convenience of city living.

○ The entertainment options in cities are unparalleled, from cinemas and concert halls to nightclubs, sports arenas, and live performances. The constant availability of activities and events ensures that there is always something to do, making urban life exciting and fulfilling for residents of all ages.

○ The ability to participate in a wide range of activities, from cultural and recreational to professional and educational, gives urban residents a sense of autonomy and freedom that is often limited in rural areas. This access to a broader spectrum of experiences and opportunities is a key factor in the allure of city life.

In conclusion, the attraction of cities is driven by a combination of economic opportunities, access to quality education and healthcare, and the cultural and social pull of urban life. These factors collectively make cities desirable places to live, work, and thrive, contributing to the ongoing trend of rural-to-urban migration. As urban centres continue to grow and evolve, understanding these dynamics will be crucial for addressing the challenges and opportunities that arise from the concentration of populations in cities.

Chapter 6: The Gentrification Debate

Benefits of Gentrification: Urban Renewal, Increased Property Values, and Economic Growth

Gentrification, while often controversial, is associated with several benefits that can contribute to the revitalization of urban neighbourhoods and broader economic growth. Proponents of gentrification argue that it can lead to urban renewal, increased property values, and a more vibrant local economy.

1. **Urban Renewal:**

   o Gentrification often begins with the physical transformation of neglected urban areas. As new residents and developers invest in these neighbourhoods, they restore and renovate old buildings, improve infrastructure, and enhance public spaces. This process of urban renewal can breathe new life into decaying areas, making them more attractive and safer for residents.

   o The aesthetic improvements that accompany gentrification—such as cleaner streets, better-maintained parks, and renovated homes—can enhance the overall quality of life for residents. Public and private investments often lead to the creation of new amenities like cafes, shops, and cultural spaces, contributing to a more vibrant community environment.

   o Urban renewal through gentrification can also address issues like crime and blight. As neighbourhoods become more desirable and populated, there is often a decrease in crime rates and an increase in community engagement, leading to a safer and more cohesive urban environment.

2. **Increased Property Values**:

○ One of the most immediate and tangible benefits of gentrification is the increase in property values. As demand for housing in gentrifying neighbourhoods rises, property prices and rents tend to go up. For homeowners and landlords, this can result in significant financial gains, as their assets appreciate in value.

○ Higher property values can also lead to an increase in local tax revenues, which can be reinvested in public services and infrastructure. This, in turn, can improve the quality of schools, transportation, and public safety in the neighbourhood, creating a positive feedback loop that further enhances the area's desirability.

○ The rising property values associated with gentrification can also stimulate further investment in the area. Developers and investors are more likely to finance new housing projects, commercial developments, and other ventures in neighbourhoods where property values are on the rise, contributing to the area's economic vitality.

3. **Economic Growth**:

○ Gentrification can stimulate local economic growth by attracting new businesses and creating jobs. As new residents with higher incomes move into gentrifying neighbourhoods, demand for goods and services increases, leading to the opening of new shops, restaurants, and other businesses.

○ The influx of capital and consumer spending associated with gentrification can revitalise local economies, creating employment opportunities for both new and existing residents. Additionally, the presence of new businesses can help diversify the local economy, making it more resilient to economic downturns.

○ Gentrification can also attract tourists and visitors, particularly in cities where gentrified neighbourhoods become cultural or entertainment hotspots. This can generate additional revenue for local businesses and contribute to the city's overall economic health.

Negative Consequences: Displacement, Social Inequality, and Loss of Cultural Identity

Despite its potential benefits, gentrification is often criticised for its negative consequences, particularly its impact on long-term residents and the social fabric of neighbourhoods. The most significant drawbacks of gentrification include displacement, social inequality, and the loss of cultural identity.

1. **Displacement:**

○ One of the most contentious aspects of gentrification is the displacement of long-term residents. As property values and rents rise, many low-income residents find themselves unable to afford their homes and are forced to move to more affordable areas. This displacement can lead to the breakdown of tight-knit communities and the loss of social networks that have developed over years or even generations.

○ Displacement can disproportionately affect vulnerable populations, including the elderly, minorities, and low-income families. These groups often have fewer resources and options when it comes to relocating, and the process of displacement can be particularly disruptive to their lives.

○ The displacement caused by gentrification can also contribute to housing instability and homelessness. As affordable housing becomes scarcer in gentrifying neighbourhoods, displaced residents may struggle to find new homes within their budget, leading to increased rates of homelessness and housing insecurity.

2. Social Inequality:

○ Gentrification can exacerbate existing social inequalities by creating divisions between new, often wealthier residents and the long-term, lower-income residents. The influx of more affluent individuals can drive up the cost of living in the neighbourhood, making it difficult for existing residents to afford basic goods and services.

○ The economic disparities between new and old residents can lead to social tensions and a sense of alienation among long-term residents. As gentrifying neighbourhoods become more expensive and exclusive, the original residents may feel marginalised and excluded from the benefits of the neighbourhood's revitalization.

○ Gentrification can also result in a loss of affordable housing options. As landlords and developers convert or replace affordable housing with luxury apartments or condominiums, low-income residents may be pushed out of the neighbourhood entirely, leading to greater economic and social segregation within cities.

3. Loss of Cultural Identity:

○ Gentrification can lead to the erosion of the cultural identity and heritage of neighbourhoods. Many urban areas have deep-rooted cultural traditions and histories that are closely tied to the communities that have lived there for generations. As new residents move in and old residents are displaced, the unique character of these neighbourhoods can be lost.

○ The commercialization and homogenization that often accompany gentrification can further dilute the cultural identity of neighbourhoods. As independent businesses and cultural institutions are replaced by chain stores and high-end boutiques, the distinctiveness of the neighbourhood may be replaced by a more generic, mainstream urban culture.

○ The loss of cultural identity can also manifest in the erasure of historical landmarks and community spaces. In the pursuit of development and modernization, historic buildings, cultural centres, and places of worship that once served as pillars of the community may be demolished or repurposed, leading to a loss of collective memory and heritage.

Case Studies: Examining Gentrification in Cities like New York, London, and Berlin

To fully understand the complexities of gentrification, it is essential to examine specific case studies from cities around the world. New York, London, and Berlin are three cities that have experienced significant gentrification, each with its own unique dynamics and outcomes.

1. **New York City:**

○ In New York City, gentrification has been most prominent in neighbourhoods like Harlem, Williamsburg, and the Lower East Side. These areas, once characterised by economic hardship and high crime rates, have undergone dramatic transformations over the past few decades.

○ In Harlem, for example, gentrification has brought an influx of new businesses, luxury apartments, and affluent residents. While this has led to economic growth and urban renewal, it has also displaced many of the neighbourhood's long-term residents, particularly African American and Hispanic communities that have historically called Harlem home.

○ The gentrification of Williamsburg in Brooklyn is another notable example. Once an industrial area with a large working-class population, Williamsburg has become one of New York's trendiest neighbourhoods, attracting artists, young professionals, and tech entrepreneurs. However, this transformation has come at the cost of rising rents and the displacement of the neighborhood's original residents, leading to tensions and debates over the impact of gentrification on community cohesion.

2. **London**:

○ In London, the process of gentrification has been particularly evident in neighbourhoods like Brixton, Shoreditch, and Hackney. These areas, once known for their diverse and vibrant working-class communities, have seen significant changes as new, wealthier residents have moved in and property values have soared.

○ Brixton, a historically Afro-Caribbean neighbourhood, has experienced rapid gentrification, leading to the displacement of many long-term residents and the loss of some of the area's cultural landmarks. While the influx of investment has revitalised the area, bringing new businesses and improving infrastructure, it has also sparked debates about the erasure of Brixton's cultural identity and the widening gap between rich and poor residents.

○ Shoreditch, once a hub for artists and creative industries, has also undergone significant gentrification. The area has transformed into a fashionable district, with trendy bars, restaurants, and tech companies replacing the old warehouses and industrial spaces. While this has boosted the local economy, it has also led to the displacement of artists and low-income residents who can no longer afford to live in the area.

3. **Berlin**:

○ Berlin's experience with gentrification is somewhat unique, given the city's history and its reputation as a haven for artists, students, and activists. Neighbourhoods like Kreuzberg, Prenzlauer Berg, and Neukölln have seen waves of gentrification, driven by both domestic and international migration.

○ Prenzlauer Berg, once a working-class district in East Berlin, has become one of the city's most desirable neighbourhoods, attracting young professionals and families. The area's transformation has been marked by the renovation of old buildings, the opening of upscale cafes and boutiques, and a dramatic increase in property values. However, this has also led to the displacement of many long-term residents, particularly those who lived in the area during the days of East Berlin.

○ Kreuzberg, known for its countercultural scene and large immigrant population, has also been affected by gentrification. The influx of new residents and the commercialization of the neighbourhood have sparked protests and resistance from local communities, who fear the loss of Kreuzberg's unique identity and the displacement of its diverse population.

In summary, the gentrification debate is complex and multifaceted, with both positive and negative consequences for urban neighbourhoods. While gentrification can lead to urban renewal, increased property values, and economic growth, it can also result in displacement, social inequality, and the loss of cultural identity. By examining case studies from cities like New York, London, and Berlin.

Chapter 7: Rural Communities in Transition

Strategies for Revitalising Rural Areas: Economic Diversification and Sustainable Development

Rural communities around the world face significant challenges as they grapple with economic stagnation, depopulation, and the loss of traditional industries. However, there are strategies that can help revitalise these areas, ensuring their long-term sustainability and resilience. Economic diversification and sustainable development are two key approaches that can transform rural communities, making them more vibrant and economically viable.

1. **Economic Diversification:**

    ○ Economic diversification is essential for the survival and growth of rural communities. Traditionally reliant on a single industry—such as agriculture, mining, or manufacturing—many rural areas have been left vulnerable to economic downturns and shifts in global markets. Diversifying the local economy can help mitigate these risks and create a more stable economic base.

    ○ One approach to economic diversification is to develop new industries that build on the strengths of the local area. For example, rural regions with natural beauty and outdoor recreational opportunities can develop tourism and eco-tourism industries, attracting visitors and creating jobs in hospitality, guiding, and conservation.

○ Another strategy is to invest in small and medium-sized enterprises (SMEs) that can provide employment and stimulate local economic growth. Encouraging entrepreneurship and supporting local businesses through grants, training programs, and access to capital can help create a more dynamic and resilient rural economy.

○ Additionally, the promotion of value-added agriculture—such as organic farming, artisanal food production, and agritourism—can help rural communities capitalise on their agricultural heritage while adapting to changing consumer preferences. These new industries can provide a higher return on investment than traditional commodity farming, helping to sustain rural livelihoods.

2. Sustainable Development:

○ Sustainable development is critical to the long-term health of rural communities. It involves managing natural resources in a way that meets current needs without compromising the ability of future generations to meet their own needs. For rural areas, this often means balancing economic development with environmental stewardship and social equity.

○ One aspect of sustainable development is the promotion of renewable energy sources, such as wind, solar, and bioenergy. Rural areas, with their abundant land and natural resources, are well-positioned to become leaders in renewable energy production. Developing renewable energy projects can create jobs, generate revenue, and reduce reliance on fossil fuels, contributing to both economic and environmental sustainability.

○ Sustainable agriculture practices, such as crop rotation, organic farming, and conservation tillage, can help preserve soil health, water quality, and biodiversity, ensuring that rural lands remain productive for generations to come. These practices can also make farming more resilient to climate change, reducing the risk of crop failures and economic losses.

○ Community-based conservation efforts, where local residents are actively involved in managing and protecting natural resources, can also play a key role in sustainable rural development. These initiatives can help preserve critical ecosystems, protect wildlife, and maintain the cultural and recreational value of rural landscapes.

3. Education and Workforce Development:

○ Investing in education and workforce development is another crucial strategy for revitalising rural areas. As traditional industries decline, rural communities need to equip their residents with the skills and knowledge required to participate in the modern economy.

○ Expanding access to vocational training, technical education, and higher education opportunities in rural areas can help residents develop the skills needed for new industries and emerging job markets. Online education and distance learning programs can also play a role in bridging the educational gap between urban and rural areas.

○ Partnerships between local governments, educational institutions, and businesses can create pathways for rural residents to enter high-demand fields, such as healthcare, information technology, and renewable energy. By aligning educational programs with the needs of the local economy, rural communities can create a more skilled and adaptable workforce.

The Role of Technology in Bridging the Urban-Rural Divide

Technology has the potential to bridge the urban-rural divide by connecting rural communities to the broader economy, improving access to services, and enhancing the quality of life. From broadband internet access to telemedicine and e-commerce, technological advancements are transforming rural areas and helping them compete in the global economy.

1. **Broadband Internet Access**:

○ High-speed internet is a critical infrastructure for modern life, yet many rural areas still lack reliable broadband access. Expanding broadband infrastructure in rural areas is essential for economic development, education, healthcare, and social connectivity.

○ Access to broadband internet enables rural businesses to reach new markets, participate in e-commerce, and compete on a level playing field with urban counterparts. It also allows residents to work remotely, access online education, and engage in telemedicine, reducing the need to travel long distances for work, study, or healthcare.

○ Governments, private companies, and non-profit organisations can work together to invest in rural broadband infrastructure, ensuring that rural communities have the connectivity they need to thrive in the digital age.

Public-private partnerships, subsidies, and grants can help make broadband access more affordable and widespread in rural areas.

2. Telemedicine and Healthcare Access:

○ Telemedicine is revolutionising healthcare delivery in rural areas, where access to medical services is often limited. Through telemedicine, rural residents can consult with doctors, specialists, and mental health professionals without having to travel to distant cities.

○ Telemedicine can help address the shortage of healthcare providers in rural areas by connecting patients with a wider network of medical professionals. This can be particularly important for managing chronic conditions, providing mental health services, and offering specialised care that may not be available locally.

○ The use of mobile health technologies, such as remote monitoring devices and health apps, can also improve healthcare outcomes in rural areas by enabling continuous monitoring and early intervention for patients with chronic diseases. This can reduce the burden on local healthcare facilities and improve the overall health of rural populations.

3. E-commerce and Rural Businesses:

○ E-commerce provides rural businesses with an opportunity to reach a global customer base, bypassing the limitations of local markets. Through online platforms, rural entrepreneurs can sell products and services to customers around the world, expanding their business opportunities and increasing revenue.

○ The rise of e-commerce has also led to the growth of niche markets and artisanal goods, allowing rural producers to capitalise on the demand for unique, handcrafted, and locally-sourced products. This can create new income streams for rural residents and support the preservation of traditional crafts and agricultural practices.

○ Technology can also enhance the efficiency and productivity of rural businesses through the use of digital tools, such as online marketing, inventory management software, and customer relationship management systems. By adopting these technologies, rural businesses can improve their operations, reduce costs, and better serve their customers.

The Future of Rural Communities: Adaptation or Decline?

The future of rural communities will largely depend on their ability to adapt to changing economic, social, and environmental conditions. While some rural areas may continue to struggle with depopulation and economic decline, others have the potential to thrive by embracing new opportunities and innovative approaches to development.

1. **Adaptation through Innovation**:

○ Rural communities that embrace innovation and diversification are more likely to succeed in the future. By adopting new technologies, exploring alternative industries, and investing in education and workforce development, these communities can build a more resilient and sustainable economic base.

○ The success of rural areas will also depend on their ability to attract and retain residents, particularly young people and families. Offering a high quality of life, affordable housing, and access to amenities and services can help rural communities compete with urban areas for talent and investment.

○ Collaboration between rural communities, government agencies, and private sector partners will be essential for driving innovation and ensuring that rural areas have the resources and support they need to thrive. Regional cooperation and knowledge-sharing can help rural communities learn from each other's successes and avoid common pitfalls.

2. **Challenges to Adaptation**:

○ Despite the potential for adaptation, many rural communities face significant challenges that may hinder their ability to thrive. These challenges include ageing populations, limited access to capital, infrastructure deficits, and environmental pressures such as climate change.

○ The outmigration of young people and the decline of traditional industries can create a cycle of decline, where shrinking populations lead to reduced economic activity, which in turn exacerbates population loss. Breaking this cycle will require targeted interventions and sustained investment in rural areas.

○ Environmental challenges, such as extreme weather events, soil degradation, and water scarcity, can also threaten the viability of rural communities, particularly those reliant on agriculture and natural resources. Addressing these challenges will require a focus on sustainability and resilience in rural development planning.

3. Scenarios for the Future:

○ The future of rural communities could unfold in several different ways, depending on how effectively they respond to the challenges and opportunities they face. In some cases, rural areas may experience a resurgence, driven by innovation, technology, and sustainable development practices. These communities could become models of rural resilience, attracting new residents and investment while preserving their cultural heritage and natural environments.

○ Alternatively, some rural areas may continue to experience decline, particularly if they are unable to diversify their economies or attract new residents. These communities may face ongoing depopulation, economic stagnation, and the erosion of social and cultural institutions.

○ Ultimately, the future of rural communities will depend on the choices made by residents, policymakers, and stakeholders today. By focusing on adaptation, innovation, and sustainability, rural areas can chart a course toward a more prosperous and resilient future.

In conclusion, rural communities are at a crossroads, facing both significant challenges and exciting opportunities. Through strategies like economic diversification, sustainable development, and the adoption of new technologies, rural areas can revitalise themselves and ensure a brighter future. The success of these efforts will determine whether rural communities adapt and thrive or continue to struggle with decline in the years to come.

Chapter 8: Urban Planning and Policy Responses

Urban Policy Responses to Gentrification: Affordable Housing, Rent Control, and Inclusionary Zoning

Gentrification presents a complex challenge for urban policymakers, who must balance the need for economic development and urban renewal with the imperative to protect vulnerable populations from displacement and ensure equitable access to housing. Several policy tools have been developed and implemented in cities worldwide to address the impacts of gentrification, including affordable housing initiatives, rent control, and inclusionary zoning.

1. **Affordable Housing Initiatives**:

   ○ Affordable housing is one of the most crucial components of urban policy aimed at mitigating the negative effects of gentrification. Ensuring that long-term residents have access to affordable homes in gentrifying neighbourhoods can help prevent displacement and preserve the socioeconomic diversity of urban areas.

   ○ Governments and local authorities can invest in the construction of new affordable housing units, either through direct public investment or by providing incentives for private developers to include affordable units in their projects. These incentives can include tax breaks, grants, or subsidies that make it financially viable for developers to offer affordable housing.

○ Preservation of existing affordable housing is also critical. Policies that protect and maintain current affordable units, such as offering financial assistance for repairs and renovations, can help prevent the loss of affordable housing stock in gentrifying neighbourhoods. Additionally, housing cooperatives, land trusts, and non-profit housing organisations can play a significant role in maintaining affordable housing options over the long term.

2. Rent Control:

○ Rent control is a policy tool designed to limit the rate at which landlords can increase rents, thereby providing greater stability and affordability for tenants in rapidly gentrifying areas. By capping rent increases, rent control aims to protect long-term residents from being priced out of their homes as property values rise.

○ While rent control can be effective in preventing sudden rent hikes, it is often a controversial policy, with critics arguing that it can discourage investment in rental housing, reduce the overall supply of rental units, and lead to the deterioration of existing properties. Policymakers must carefully design rent control measures to strike a balance between protecting tenants and encouraging the continued development of rental housing.

○ Some cities have implemented variations of rent control, such as rent stabilisation, which allows for modest rent increases tied to inflation or other economic indicators. These policies can provide a middle ground, offering protections for tenants while still allowing for some flexibility in the rental market.

3. Inclusionary Zoning:

○ Inclusionary zoning is a policy that requires or incentivizes developers to include a certain percentage of affordable housing units within new residential developments. This approach aims to create mixed-income communities and ensure that affordable housing is integrated into all parts of a city, including rapidly gentrifying neighbourhoods.

○ Inclusionary zoning can take various forms, ranging from mandatory requirements to voluntary programs that offer developers incentives such as increased density allowances, expedited permitting, or tax abatements in exchange for including affordable units in their projects.

○ One of the strengths of inclusionary zoning is that it leverages private sector development to address the need for affordable housing, reducing the financial burden on public resources. However, the effectiveness of inclusionary zoning policies depends on careful design, including setting the right affordability thresholds and ensuring that the policies are flexible enough to adapt to local housing market conditions.

Balancing Growth and Equity: Lessons from Global Cities

As cities around the world grapple with the challenges of gentrification, there are valuable lessons to be learned from global experiences in balancing economic growth with social equity. The following examples highlight some of the strategies that have been employed to ensure that urban development benefits all residents, not just the affluent.

1. Barcelona, Spain:

○ Barcelona has implemented a comprehensive set of policies aimed at addressing gentrification and promoting social equity in urban development. The city's approach includes a strong emphasis on affordable housing, with a significant portion of new residential developments required to be set aside for social housing.

○ The city has also implemented measures to protect small businesses and local culture, recognizing that gentrification often threatens the unique character of neighbourhoods. By supporting local businesses through grants, favourable zoning regulations, and initiatives to preserve traditional markets, Barcelona has sought to maintain the cultural diversity and vibrancy of its neighbourhoods.

○ Additionally, Barcelona has engaged in participatory urban planning processes, involving residents in decision-making and ensuring that development plans reflect the needs and aspirations of the community. This inclusive approach has helped to build trust between residents and local authorities and has contributed to more equitable outcomes in urban development.

2. New York City, USA:

○ New York City has employed a variety of strategies to balance growth and equity in the face of intense gentrification pressures. One of the city's key tools has been the use of inclusionary zoning, which requires developers to include affordable housing units in new residential projects in exchange for zoning bonuses that allow for higher-density construction.

○ The city has also implemented programs to preserve existing affordable housing, such as rent stabilisation and subsidies for low-income tenants. These measures have helped to protect long-term residents from displacement while also encouraging new development in underutilised areas.

○ New York City has also experimented with community land trusts, where land is held in trust by a non-profit organisation to ensure that it remains affordable for residents. This model has been particularly effective in preserving affordable housing in rapidly gentrifying neighbourhoods like the Lower East Side and East Harlem.

3. Copenhagen, Denmark:

○ Copenhagen is known for its commitment to social equity and sustainability in urban development. The city has adopted a mixed-use, mixed-income approach to housing, where public housing is integrated with private developments, ensuring that all residents have access to high-quality living environments.

○ The city's urban planning policies prioritise green spaces, public transportation, and community amenities, creating neighbourhoods that are not only economically vibrant but also socially inclusive. Copenhagen's approach to gentrification focuses on creating balanced communities where people of all income levels can live, work, and play.

○ Copenhagen's success in balancing growth and equity is also due to its strong tradition of citizen participation in urban planning. The city engages residents in the planning process through public consultations, workshops, and participatory budgeting, ensuring that development plans reflect the needs and values of the community.

The Role of Local Governments and Community Activism

Local governments and community activism play a crucial role in shaping the outcomes of gentrification. While policymakers are responsible for designing and implementing policies that address the impacts of gentrification, community activism is essential for ensuring that these policies are responsive to the needs of residents and that they are effectively enforced.

1. **Local Governments**:

○ Local governments are at the forefront of the battle against the negative consequences of gentrification. They have the power to enact and enforce policies that can protect residents from displacement, promote affordable housing, and ensure that urban development is equitable and inclusive.

○ One of the most important roles of local governments is to create and implement comprehensive urban plans that address both the economic and social needs of the city. These plans should include strategies for managing gentrification, such as zoning regulations, affordable housing mandates, and community benefits agreements that require developers to contribute to local infrastructure and services.

○ Local governments can also foster partnerships with non-profit organisations, community groups, and private sector stakeholders to create more holistic and effective responses to gentrification. By working together, these entities can pool resources, share expertise, and develop innovative solutions to the complex challenges of urban development.

2. Community Activism:

○ Community activism is a powerful force in the fight against the negative impacts of gentrification. Grassroots movements, tenant organisations, and advocacy groups have been instrumental in raising awareness about the consequences of gentrification and pushing for policies that protect vulnerable residents.

○ Activists often organise around issues such as affordable housing, tenants' rights, and the preservation of cultural heritage. Through protests, public campaigns, and legal action, they hold local governments and developers accountable and ensure that the voices of long-term residents are heard in the planning process.

○ Community activism also plays a key role in building solidarity among residents and fostering a sense of collective ownership over the future of their neighbourhoods. By empowering residents to participate in decision-making, activism helps to create more inclusive and resilient communities that can better withstand the pressures of gentrification.

○ One notable example of community activism in action is the movement for community land trusts, which has gained momentum in cities like New York, San Francisco, and Boston. These trusts allow communities to collectively own and manage land, ensuring that it remains affordable and accessible to residents. This model has been effective in countering the forces of gentrification and preserving the social fabric of neighbourhoods.

3. Challenges and Opportunities:

○ Both local governments and community activists face significant challenges in addressing gentrification. These include limited financial resources, political opposition, and the complexities of balancing competing interests in urban development. However, these challenges also present opportunities for innovation and collaboration.

○ One opportunity lies in the increasing recognition of the importance of social equity in urban planning. As cities around the world grapple with the consequences of gentrification, there is growing momentum behind policies and practices that prioritise the needs of all residents, particularly the most vulnerable.

○ Another opportunity is the potential for new technologies and data-driven approaches to enhance the effectiveness of urban policies and community activism. For example, digital tools can be used to map gentrification trends, monitor housing affordability, and engage residents in the planning process. By leveraging technology, local governments and activists can develop more targeted and responsive strategies to address the challenges of gentrification.

In conclusion, urban planning and policy responses to gentrification must strike a delicate balance between fostering growth and ensuring equity. Through the implementation of policies like affordable housing initiatives, rent control, and inclusionary zoning, cities can protect vulnerable populations and promote social inclusion. Additionally, by learning from global examples and supporting community activism, local governments can create more resilient and equitable

Chapter 9: Global Perspectives on Gentrification and Migration

Gentrification in Emerging Economies: The Case of China, India, and Brazil

Gentrification is not limited to developed economies; it is also a significant phenomenon in emerging economies where rapid urbanisation and economic growth create new dynamics in urban development. In countries like China, India, and Brazil, gentrification manifests in unique ways, influenced by local economic, social, and cultural factors.

1. **China:**

   o **Urban Redevelopment**: In China, gentrification is often driven by large-scale urban redevelopment projects. Cities like Shanghai, Beijing, and Guangzhou have seen significant transformations as old neighbourhoods are demolished and replaced with modern high-rises and commercial developments. This process is often part of broader efforts to modernise and attract international investment.

   o **Economic Displacement**: The redevelopment projects frequently result in the displacement of low-income residents, who are often relocated to peripheral areas or more affordable housing developments. The rapid pace of construction and the scale of redevelopment can lead to social dislocation and a loss of community networks.

   o **Cultural Shifts**: As urban areas gentrify, they often become more oriented towards affluent lifestyles, with an emphasis on luxury retail, high-end restaurants, and cultural attractions. This shift can erode local cultural heritage and traditional lifestyles, leading to tensions between new and existing residents.

2. India:

○ **Property Development and Infrastructure**: In Indian cities such as Mumbai, Bangalore, and Delhi, gentrification is driven by property developers and infrastructure projects aimed at improving urban environments and attracting investment. The development of upscale residential complexes and commercial centres is often concentrated in historically underdeveloped areas.

○ **Social Impact**: The influx of higher-income residents and the renovation of urban spaces can lead to the displacement of poorer communities. In cities with high population densities and limited affordable housing options, the impact of gentrification can be particularly severe, exacerbating existing inequalities.

○ **Urban Policy**: Indian cities are grappling with how to manage gentrification in ways that balance development with social equity. Some cities are exploring policies to include affordable housing in new developments and to improve the conditions of informal settlements, but challenges remain in implementing and enforcing these policies.

3. Brazil:

○ **Economic Development and Social Exclusion**: In Brazilian cities like São Paulo and Rio de Janeiro, gentrification is linked to economic development and the expansion of middle-class neighbourhoods. Redevelopment projects often focus on improving infrastructure and creating commercial hubs, leading to the displacement of low-income residents.

○ **Favela Upgrading**: Brazil has also seen efforts to upgrade informal settlements, known as favelas, to improve living conditions and integrate them into the urban fabric. While these efforts can provide better housing and infrastructure, they can also lead to increased property values and the displacement of original residents.

○ **Community Responses**: Activist groups and community organisations in Brazil play a crucial role in advocating for the rights of displaced residents and in pushing for inclusive urban policies. These groups often work to ensure that redevelopment projects include provisions for affordable housing and support for affected communities.

Migration and Urbanization in the Global South

Migration and urbanisation in the Global South present unique challenges and opportunities as rapidly growing cities strive to accommodate expanding populations and improve living conditions. The interplay between migration and urban growth is influenced by various factors, including economic development, political instability, and environmental changes.

1. **Rapid Urban Growth**:

○ Many cities in the Global South are experiencing unprecedented rates of urban growth due to both internal migration from rural areas and international migration from neighbouring countries. This rapid urbanisation can strain existing infrastructure and services, leading to challenges in providing adequate housing, transportation, and healthcare.

○ Informal settlements or slums often emerge in response to the lack of affordable housing, leading to overcrowded living conditions and inadequate access to basic services. Addressing these challenges requires comprehensive urban planning and investment in infrastructure to improve living conditions for all residents.

2. Economic Opportunities:

○ Urbanisation in the Global South is often driven by the search for economic opportunities, with migrants moving to cities in hopes of finding better employment prospects and improved quality of life. However, the informal economy frequently absorbs a large portion of the migrant population, leading to precarious working conditions and limited access to social protections.

○ Economic development policies that focus on job creation, skills training, and support for small businesses can help improve economic opportunities for urban migrants. Investing in education and vocational training programs can also enhance the employability of migrants and support their integration into the formal economy.

3. Political and Environmental Factors:

○ Political instability, conflict, and environmental changes can drive migration and exacerbate urbanisation pressures. For example, displacement due to conflict or natural disasters can lead to sudden increases in urban populations, creating additional challenges for city planners and policymakers.

○ Addressing these issues requires a coordinated response that includes humanitarian assistance, disaster relief, and long-term strategies for integrating displaced populations into urban areas. International cooperation and support from non-governmental organisations can play a crucial role in managing the impacts of forced migration and ensuring that affected communities receive the necessary support.

Comparative Analysis: Gentrification in Different Cultural and Economic Contexts

Gentrification manifests differently across various cultural and economic contexts, shaped by local histories, socio-economic conditions, and urban policies. A comparative analysis reveals how different cities navigate the challenges and opportunities associated with gentrification.

1. **Cultural Contexts**:

○ **Cultural Heritage and Identity**: In cities with rich cultural histories, such as Paris and Istanbul, gentrification can impact the preservation of cultural heritage and local identity. The influx of affluent residents and new developments can alter the character of neighbourhoods and lead to the displacement of traditional communities.

○ **Local Responses**: Cities with strong cultural traditions may implement policies to protect historic districts and support local businesses, such as heritage conservation programs and cultural districts. These measures aim to preserve the unique cultural identity of neighbourhoods while accommodating economic development.

2. Economic Contexts:

○ **Developed Economies**: In developed economies, such as those in Western Europe and North America, gentrification often involves high-end residential and commercial development, driven by property markets and investment. Policies may focus on mitigating the displacement of low-income residents through affordable housing programs and rent control.

○ **Emerging Economies**: In emerging economies, gentrification can be driven by rapid economic growth and infrastructure development. The focus may be on addressing the challenges of informal settlements and integrating new developments with existing communities. Policies in these contexts often aim to balance economic growth with social inclusion and access to basic services.

3. Policy Approaches:

○ **Inclusive Development**: Cities that successfully manage gentrification often adopt inclusive development approaches that integrate affordable housing, community engagement, and economic opportunities for all residents. Policies may include mixed-income housing, community land trusts, and participatory planning processes.

○ **Adaptive Strategies**: In cities facing rapid urbanisation and gentrification pressures, adaptive strategies are essential for addressing the unique challenges of each context. This may involve tailoring policies to local conditions, engaging with affected communities, and fostering collaboration between stakeholders.

In conclusion, understanding gentrification and migration from a global perspective highlights the diverse ways in which cities address the complexities of urban development. By examining case studies from different cultural and economic contexts, policymakers and planners can gain insights into effective strategies for managing gentrification, promoting equitable growth, and ensuring that urbanisation benefits all residents.

Chapter 10: Socioeconomic and Cultural Impacts

The Changing Urban Landscape: Architecture, Public Spaces, and Neighborhood Dynamics

Gentrification significantly transforms the urban landscape, affecting architecture, public spaces, and the dynamics of neighbourhoods. These changes can reshape the physical and social fabric of cities, leading to both positive and negative outcomes.

1. **Architecture and Urban Design**:

    ○ **Modernization and Aesthetics**: Gentrification often leads to the modernization of architectural styles and urban design. New developments typically feature contemporary designs, luxury materials, and high-end finishes, which contrast sharply with the existing architecture of older, often deteriorated buildings. This can enhance the visual appeal of neighbourhoods and attract investment but can also lead to the loss of historical and cultural architectural elements.

    ○ **Preservation vs. Innovation**: Balancing modernization with preservation is a key challenge. While new developments can revitalise areas, preserving historical and culturally significant buildings is essential for maintaining a neighbourhood's unique character. Cities often face tensions between developers pushing for contemporary designs and communities advocating for the conservation of heritage structures.

    ○ **Mixed-Use Developments**: Gentrified areas often see the rise of mixed-use developments that combine residential, commercial, and recreational spaces. These developments can create vibrant and dynamic urban environments, offering amenities such as cafes, shops, and recreational facilities. However, they can also lead to the displacement of small, local businesses in favour of more upscale, commercial enterprises.

2. **Public Spaces**:

o **Improvement and Access**: The redevelopment of gentrified neighbourhoods frequently includes improvements to public spaces, such as parks, plazas, and streetscapes. Enhanced green spaces and well-designed public areas can improve the quality of life for residents, offering opportunities for recreation, socialisation, and community engagement.

o **Gentrification and Public Space Use**: Changes in public spaces can lead to shifts in their use and accessibility. As neighbourhoods gentrify, public spaces may become more oriented towards the preferences and needs of new, higher-income residents, potentially reducing access and relevance for long-term, lower-income residents. This shift can exacerbate feelings of exclusion and undermine the inclusive role of public spaces.

o **Community Engagement**: Involving existing communities in the planning and design of public spaces is crucial for ensuring that these spaces meet the needs of all residents. Participatory design processes can help integrate diverse perspectives and create public areas that foster social cohesion and inclusivity.

3. **Neighborhood Dynamics**:

○ **Social Mixing**: Gentrification often brings together residents from different socioeconomic backgrounds, creating opportunities for social mixing and interaction. This can lead to the enrichment of community life and the creation of diverse social networks. However, it can also result in social tensions and conflicts between long-term residents and newcomers.

○ **Changing Demographics**: As neighbourhoods gentrify, there are often significant changes in demographic profiles. The influx of higher-income residents can alter the social and cultural makeup of an area, leading to shifts in community norms, values, and practices. Long-term residents may experience a sense of displacement or loss of identity as their neighbourhoods change.

○ **Economic Displacement**: The economic pressures of gentrification can lead to the displacement of lower-income residents, who may be forced to move to less desirable areas or experience increased financial strain. This displacement can disrupt community networks and social cohesion, as well as lead to increased inequality and segregation.

Social and Cultural Integration in Gentrified Areas

Social and cultural integration in gentrified areas is a complex process that involves both challenges and opportunities for fostering inclusivity and community cohesion.

1. **Integration Challenges**:

○ **Cultural Differences**: The arrival of new, often more affluent residents in gentrified areas can introduce cultural differences that may lead to tensions with long-standing community members. Differences in lifestyle, values, and social practices can create barriers to integration and mutual understanding.

○ **Exclusion and Marginalisation**: Long-term residents may feel marginalised or excluded as their neighbourhoods change. They may face difficulties accessing new amenities or services that cater primarily to the preferences of newcomers. Efforts to integrate diverse populations must address these feelings of exclusion and work to ensure that all residents have a stake in their community's development.

○ **Social Fragmentation**: Rapid social changes can lead to fragmentation within communities, where different groups remain isolated from one another rather than interacting and building relationships. This fragmentation can undermine social cohesion and reduce the effectiveness of community-building efforts.

2. **Opportunities for Integration**:

○ **Community Engagement**: Active engagement of both new and existing residents in community activities, decision-making processes, and local events can foster social integration and build a sense of shared identity. Community organisations, local events, and participatory planning processes can help bridge gaps between different groups and promote mutual understanding.

○ **Cultural Exchange**: Gentrified neighbourhoods often become melting pots of different cultures, offering opportunities for cultural exchange and enrichment. Community festivals, art projects, and cultural programs can celebrate diversity and create spaces for residents to share and appreciate each other's backgrounds and traditions.

○ **Inclusive Planning**: Inclusive urban planning that considers the needs and perspectives of all residents can facilitate social and cultural integration. By incorporating input from diverse community members and addressing the concerns of both new and long-term residents, planners can create environments that support social cohesion and inclusivity.

The Rise of Urban Inequality: Wealth Disparities and Social Tensions

Gentrification often exacerbates urban inequality, leading to significant disparities in wealth and social tensions between different groups within gentrified areas.

1. **Wealth Disparities**:

○ **Income Inequality**: Gentrification can widen income inequality as property values and living costs rise, benefiting higher-income residents while placing financial strain on lower-income individuals. The increased cost of living in gentrified neighbourhoods can lead to greater economic disparity and social stratification.

○ **Economic Segregation**: As neighbourhoods gentrify, there is often a spatial segregation of economic classes, with wealthier residents concentrated in newly developed or renovated areas and lower-income residents pushed to less desirable parts of the city. This segregation can reinforce social divides and limit opportunities for social interaction between different economic groups.

2. Social Tensions:

○ **Class Conflict**: The displacement of long-term residents and the changing character of neighbourhoods can lead to conflicts between different social classes. Long-term residents may feel that their neighbourhoods are being taken over by outsiders who do not understand or value their community's history and culture.

○ **Community Fragmentation**: The social and economic changes brought about by gentrification can lead to fragmentation within communities, with different groups maintaining separate spheres of social and economic activity. This fragmentation can hinder efforts to build inclusive and cohesive communities.

○ **Resistance and Activism**: In response to the negative impacts of gentrification, grassroots activism and community resistance often emerge. Residents and advocacy groups may mobilise to fight against displacement, advocate for affordable housing, and demand more equitable development practices.

In conclusion, the socioeconomic and cultural impacts of gentrification are multifaceted, affecting the urban landscape, public spaces, and neighbourhood dynamics in profound ways. Understanding these impacts and addressing the associated challenges requires a comprehensive approach that includes inclusive planning, community engagement, and efforts to mitigate inequality. By fostering social integration and addressing the needs of all residents, cities can work towards more equitable and resilient urban environments.

Chapter 11: Future Trends and Projections

The Role of Technology in Shaping Future Urban Migration

Technology is poised to play a transformative role in shaping urban migration patterns and influencing how cities evolve in the coming years. Advances in technology are impacting both the push and pull factors of migration, as well as how urban environments are designed and managed.

1. **Digital Connectivity and Remote Work**:

   ○ **Remote Work Opportunities**: The rise of remote work and digital nomadism allows individuals to live anywhere while working for companies based in urban centres. This flexibility can reduce the pressure on major cities by allowing people to move to rural or less densely populated areas without sacrificing employment opportunities.

   ○ **Decentralised Workspaces**: Technology enables the creation of decentralised workspaces and co-working hubs in rural and suburban areas, which can attract people seeking a balance between urban amenities and a quieter lifestyle. These trends may help distribute population growth more evenly across regions.

2. **Smart Cities and Urban Innovation**:

   ○ **Smart Infrastructure**: The development of smart cities, which integrate advanced technologies into urban infrastructure, can improve the efficiency and livability of urban areas. Technologies such as IoT (Internet of Things), AI (Artificial Intelligence), and big data can enhance transportation, energy management, and public services, making cities more attractive and functional.

○ **Urban Planning**: Technology is transforming urban planning through data-driven insights and simulations. Planners can use technology to model future scenarios, assess the impact of new developments, and create more resilient and adaptable urban environments.

3. **Technology and Housing**:

○ **Housing Innovations**: Advances in construction technology, such as modular housing and 3D printing, can address housing shortages and affordability issues. These innovations can facilitate the development of affordable and sustainable housing options in both urban and rural areas.

○ **PropTech**: Property technology (PropTech) is revolutionising the real estate market by streamlining transactions, improving property management, and enhancing the home-buying and renting experience. These changes can influence migration patterns by making it easier for individuals to find and secure housing.

Climate Change and Its Impact on Rural-to-Urban Migration

Climate change is increasingly influencing migration patterns, with significant implications for both rural and urban areas. The impacts of climate change can drive rural-to-urban migration and shape the future development of cities.

1. **Environmental Disasters and Displacement**:

○ **Extreme Weather Events**: Rising temperatures, more frequent and severe storms, and other extreme weather events can lead to the displacement of populations from vulnerable rural areas. Flooding, droughts, and wildfires may force residents to move to urban areas in search of safety and stability.

○ **Sea-Level Rise**: Coastal areas are particularly at risk from sea-level rise, which can lead to the loss of land and infrastructure. This risk may drive migration from affected coastal regions to inland urban centres.

2. **Agricultural Decline and Economic Impact**:

○ **Reduced Agricultural Productivity**: Climate change can negatively impact agricultural productivity, leading to economic decline in rural areas that rely on farming. As agricultural jobs become scarcer, residents may migrate to cities in search of alternative employment opportunities.

○ **Rural Economies**: The economic impacts of climate change can exacerbate existing disparities between rural and urban areas, leading to increased pressure on urban infrastructure and services as rural populations migrate to cities.

3. **Urban Resilience and Adaptation**:

○ **Sustainable Urban Development**: Cities will need to develop strategies to adapt to climate change and enhance their resilience to environmental challenges. This includes investing in green infrastructure, improving energy efficiency, and preparing for the impacts of climate-related migration.

○ **Climate Migration Policies**: Policymakers will need to address the challenges of climate-induced migration through targeted policies that support both migrating populations and the communities they move to. This includes ensuring adequate housing, employment opportunities, and social services.

The Future of Gentrification: Sustainability, Inclusivity, and Social Justice

As cities continue to evolve, the future of gentrification will be shaped by the growing emphasis on sustainability, inclusivity, and social justice. Addressing the challenges associated with gentrification requires a forward-looking approach that balances development with equitable outcomes.

1. **Sustainable Development**:

○ **Green Building Practices**: The integration of sustainable building practices and green technologies in gentrified areas can contribute to environmental sustainability. This includes using energy-efficient materials, promoting renewable energy sources, and incorporating green spaces into urban design.

○ **Community Benefits**: Sustainable development should also consider the social and economic benefits for existing communities. Ensuring that redevelopment projects contribute to local well-being, such as through affordable housing and job creation, can help mitigate the negative impacts of gentrification.

2. Inclusivity and Social Equity:

○ **Affordable Housing Initiatives**: To address the issue of displacement, cities will need to implement policies that ensure the availability of affordable housing in gentrified areas. This includes strategies such as inclusionary zoning, rent control, and community land trusts.

○ **Community Engagement**: Involving residents in the planning and decision-making processes is crucial for ensuring that development projects reflect the needs and preferences of diverse communities. Participatory planning can help build consensus and foster a sense of ownership among residents.

3. Social Justice:

○ **Equitable Development**: Future approaches to gentrification should focus on promoting social justice by addressing historical inequalities and providing support for marginalised communities. This includes investing in education, healthcare, and social services to ensure that all residents have access to opportunities and resources.

○ **Policy Innovation**: Policymakers and urban planners will need to develop innovative policies and strategies that balance the goals of economic development with social equity. This may involve revising zoning laws, creating economic incentives for inclusive development, and fostering collaboration between public and private sectors.

In conclusion, the future of urban migration and gentrification will be shaped by technological advancements, climate change, and evolving priorities around sustainability and social justice. By addressing these trends proactively and adopting inclusive and equitable approaches, cities can navigate the challenges of urban transformation and work towards creating more resilient, fair, and vibrant urban environments.

Chapter 12: Conclusion

Summarising the Complexities of Gentrification and Rural-to-Urban Migration

Gentrification and rural-to-urban migration are complex phenomena that intertwine economic, social, and cultural dimensions, significantly impacting urban and rural landscapes. Understanding these complexities is crucial for addressing the challenges and opportunities they present.

1. **Complex Interplay:**

   o **Gentrification** involves the transformation of urban neighbourhoods through redevelopment, attracting higher-income residents and often leading to the displacement of lower-income communities. This process reshapes architectural landscapes, public spaces, and neighbourhood dynamics, leading to both revitalization and social tensions.

   o **Rural-to-Urban Migration** is driven by factors such as economic opportunities, educational prospects, and environmental challenges. As rural residents move to cities, they contribute to urban growth while facing challenges such as integration into urban environments and access to services.

2. **Dual Impact:**

   o **Urban Areas**: Gentrification can revitalise declining neighbourhoods, improve infrastructure, and attract investment. However, it also risks increasing social inequality, displacing long-term residents, and eroding cultural identities. Urban migration can lead to more vibrant and diverse cities but also strains infrastructure and services.

○ **Rural Areas**: Migration can exacerbate issues of depopulation, economic decline, and ageing populations in rural areas. Conversely, technology and sustainable development strategies offer potential pathways for revitalising rural communities and bridging the urban-rural divide.

Policy Recommendations for Equitable Urban Development

To address the challenges of gentrification and rural-to-urban migration while promoting equitable development, several policy recommendations can be considered:

1. **Affordable Housing**:

○ **Inclusionary Zoning**: Implement policies that require new developments to include affordable housing units to ensure that low- and moderate-income residents can remain in gentrifying neighbourhoods.

○ **Rent Control and Stabilization**: Introduce or strengthen rent control measures to protect existing residents from displacement due to rising housing costs.

2. **Community Engagement and Participation**:

○ **Participatory Planning**: Engage communities in the urban planning process to ensure that development projects reflect the needs and preferences of all residents, including long-term and marginalised communities.

○ **Local Empowerment**: Support community-led initiatives and organisations that advocate for equitable development and address the impacts of gentrification.

3. Economic and Social Support:

○ **Job Creation and Training**: Invest in job creation programs and vocational training to help residents adapt to changing economic conditions and benefit from new opportunities created by urban development.

○ **Support for Small Businesses**: Provide support for local businesses and entrepreneurs to ensure that they can thrive amidst gentrification and contribute to the economic diversity of neighbourhoods.

4. Sustainable Development:

○ **Green Infrastructure**: Incorporate sustainable practices and green infrastructure in urban redevelopment to promote environmental sustainability and enhance the quality of life for all residents.

○ **Climate Resilience**: Develop strategies to address the impacts of climate change on both urban and rural areas, including measures to adapt to environmental challenges and support affected populations.

Reflections on the Future of Cities and Rural Areas

The future of cities and rural areas will be shaped by ongoing trends and emerging challenges, requiring a forward-thinking approach to urban and rural development.

1. Urban Transformation:

○ **Smart Cities**: The integration of technology and innovation will continue to transform urban environments, improving efficiency and livability. Future cities will need to balance technological advancements with social equity and inclusivity.

○ **Social Justice**: Ensuring that urban development benefits all residents and addresses historical inequalities will be crucial for fostering inclusive and equitable cities.

2. Rural Revitalization:

○ **Technology and Innovation**: Advances in technology offer opportunities for revitalising rural areas, bridging the urban-rural divide, and creating new economic prospects. Emphasising sustainability and local empowerment can support long-term rural development.

○ **Adaptation Strategies**: Rural communities will need to adapt to changing economic and environmental conditions, leveraging innovation and collaboration to build resilience and ensure a vibrant future.

In conclusion, navigating the complexities of gentrification and rural-to-urban migration requires a comprehensive understanding of the interrelated factors influencing urban and rural landscapes. By implementing equitable policies, engaging communities, and embracing sustainable development, cities and rural areas can work towards creating resilient and inclusive environments that benefit all residents. The future of urban and rural areas will depend on our ability to address current challenges while fostering innovation and collaboration for a more equitable and sustainable future.

Migration Dynamics: Balancing Positive Economic Impacts with Worker Exploitation

Introduction

Migration is a powerful and multifaceted phenomenon that shapes economies and societies around the world. This book seeks to illuminate the dual facets of migration: its positive economic impacts and the often-overlooked challenges related to worker exploitation. On one hand, migration can drive economic growth, innovation, and cultural enrichment. On the other hand, it can also lead to the exploitation of vulnerable workers, who may face severe labour abuses and harsh working conditions.

The primary purpose of this book is to provide a comprehensive analysis of these contrasting aspects. By examining the ways in which migration contributes to economic vitality and the methods by which it can also result in worker exploitation, this book aims to offer a balanced perspective on the complex dynamics of modern migration. We will explore the mechanisms through which migration fosters economic development, how integration policies can enhance these benefits, and the steps necessary to address and mitigate the negative consequences faced by migrant workers.

Scope and Approach

To address this dual focus, this book is structured into two main parts:

1. **Migration's Economic Impact**: This section delves into the positive contributions of migration to economic growth. We will explore how migrants fill crucial labour gaps, contribute to innovation, and help address demographic challenges such as ageing populations. Through historical context and case studies, we will highlight success stories and examine the factors that have led to positive outcomes.

2. **Challenges of Worker Exploitation**: The second part of the

book shifts focus to the darker side of migration. It will address various forms of worker exploitation, including wage theft, unsafe working conditions, and human trafficking. This section will scrutinise the vulnerabilities of migrant workers, particularly those in undocumented or low-skilled positions, and analyse the systemic issues that allow such exploitation to persist.

Each chapter will combine theoretical analysis with practical examples to provide a nuanced understanding of migration's impact. We will also explore existing legal frameworks and policies aimed at protecting workers, and discuss strategies for creating more equitable and inclusive migration systems.

By examining both the positive and negative aspects of migration, this book aims to foster a deeper understanding of the complex interplay between economic benefits and the need for robust worker protections. It is intended for policymakers, academics, advocates, and anyone interested in the multifaceted impacts of migration on global economies and labour markets.

Chapter 1: Migration and Economic Growth

Historical Context

Migration has been a fundamental aspect of human history, shaping societies and economies across different epochs. From ancient civilizations to modern states, people have moved across regions and continents for various reasons, including trade, conflict, and economic opportunity.

- **Ancient and Mediaeval Migrations**: Early migrations, such as the movement of the Indo-Europeans, the spread of the Bantu people in Africa, and the Viking explorations, significantly influenced the development of cultures, economies, and political structures. These migrations often resulted in the exchange of goods, ideas, and technologies, contributing to economic and social development.

- **The Age of Exploration**: The 15th and 16th centuries saw significant migration due to European exploration and colonisation. This period brought about major economic changes, including the development of global trade networks and the introduction of new crops and resources to different parts of the world. However, it also had adverse effects, including the exploitation and displacement of indigenous populations.

- **Industrial Revolution and Urbanization**: The 18th and 19th centuries marked a significant increase in migration due to industrialization. People moved from rural areas to cities and from one country to another in search of industrial jobs, contributing to urban growth and economic transformation. This period also saw the rise of immigration to the Americas and Australia, driven by economic opportunities and political unrest in Europe.

- **Contemporary Migration Trends**: In recent decades, migration has been influenced by globalisation, technological advancements, and shifts in global economic patterns. Contemporary migration patterns include both voluntary movements for economic opportunities and forced migrations due to conflict and environmental changes. Understanding these historical trends provides insight into how migration has consistently impacted economies over time.

Economic Contributions

Migrants play a crucial role in driving economic growth through various mechanisms:

- **Labour Market Contributions**: Migrants often fill essential roles in labour markets that may be underserved by the native workforce. They contribute to various sectors, including agriculture, construction, healthcare, and technology. By addressing labour shortages and complementing existing skills, migrants help sustain and expand economic activity.

- **Innovation and Entrepreneurship**: Many migrants bring unique skills, perspectives, and entrepreneurial spirit to their new countries. They contribute to innovation by starting new businesses, creating jobs, and introducing new ideas and technologies. This entrepreneurial activity can stimulate economic growth and increase competitiveness in various industries.

- **Demographic and Fiscal Impact**: Migration can help counteract demographic challenges such as ageing populations and declining birth rates. By increasing the working-age population, migrants can contribute to economic growth and support public finances through their tax contributions. This is particularly important in countries facing demographic imbalances.

- **Cultural and Economic Integration**: Migrants contribute to economic growth by enhancing cultural diversity and fostering international trade and investment. Their diverse backgrounds can lead to more inclusive and creative problem-solving, which benefits various sectors of the economy.

Case Studies

● **United States**: The United States has a long history of benefiting from migration, particularly in the technology and entrepreneurial sectors. Immigrants have founded numerous successful companies, including Google, Intel, and Tesla. The U.S. also benefits from a diverse workforce that supports a wide range of industries.

● **Germany**: Germany has successfully integrated migrants into its economy, particularly in the manufacturing and healthcare sectors. The influx of skilled migrants has helped address labour shortages and contributed to the country's strong economic performance.

● **Singapore**: Singapore has leveraged migration to build a dynamic and competitive economy. The city-state has attracted skilled professionals and entrepreneurs from around the world, contributing to its status as a global financial hub and a centre for innovation.

● **Canada**: Canada's immigration policies have focused on attracting skilled workers and entrepreneurs, contributing to economic growth and innovation. The country's diverse population has also enhanced its cultural and economic vibrancy.

● **United Arab Emirates**: The UAE has utilised migrant labour to fuel its rapid economic development, particularly in construction and hospitality. While the country has seen significant economic growth, it also faces challenges related to worker exploitation, highlighting the need for effective labour protections.

These case studies illustrate the diverse ways in which migration can contribute to economic growth and highlight the importance of creating inclusive and supportive environments for migrants to maximise their positive impact.

Chapter 2: The Positive Migration Economy

Labor Market Dynamics

Migrants play a crucial role in shaping labour markets across the globe, contributing significantly to both the demand and supply sides of the economy.

- **Filling Labour Gaps**: Migrants often take on roles that are essential but hard to fill locally. These roles span various sectors, including agriculture, construction, healthcare, and service industries. By stepping into these positions, migrants help address labour shortages and maintain the functionality of critical industries. For instance, in many developed countries, migrants are vital in sectors like elder care and seasonal agriculture, where local labour is insufficient.

- **Impact on Wages and Employment**: The impact of migration on wages and employment can be complex. In some cases, an influx of migrants may lead to increased competition for low-skilled jobs, potentially suppressing wages in certain sectors. However, migrants can also drive wage increases by boosting demand for goods and services and by filling high-skilled positions that complement rather than directly compete with native workers. Additionally, the presence of migrants can lead to job creation in related sectors, such as education and training services, further benefiting the economy.

- **Sectoral Shifts**: Migrants can influence sectoral shifts within economies. For example, by providing labour for emerging industries or sectors experiencing growth, they help facilitate economic transitions and the evolution of new market trends. This dynamic can lead to more robust and flexible labour markets that adapt to changing economic conditions.

Skills and Innovation

Migrants contribute significantly to innovation and productivity through their diverse skills and perspectives.

- **Diverse Skills and Expertise**: Migrants bring a wide range of skills and expertise that can fill gaps in the local workforce. This includes high-skilled professionals in fields like technology, finance, and engineering, as well as unique skills in artisanal and creative industries. Their presence enhances the overall skill level within an economy, fostering a more competitive and diverse labour market.

- **Innovation and Creativity**: The diversity of experiences and viewpoints that migrants bring can stimulate creativity and innovation. When people from different backgrounds collaborate, they often generate new ideas and approaches that drive technological advancements and business innovations. For example, research has shown that diverse teams are more likely to produce creative solutions and perform better in problem-solving tasks.

- **Entrepreneurial Activity**: Migrants are often entrepreneurial, starting businesses at higher rates than native-born populations. These enterprises can lead to job creation, economic growth, and increased competition within markets. Notable examples include numerous tech startups founded by migrants in Silicon Valley and small businesses across urban centres that add vibrancy to local economies.

Demographic Benefits

Migration can play a key role in addressing demographic challenges faced by many countries, particularly in the context of declining birth rates and ageing populations.

- **Counteracting Population Decline**: In countries experiencing low birth rates and an ageing population, migration provides a means to sustain population levels and economic activity. By increasing the number of working-age individuals, migrants help balance demographic trends and support economic growth.

• **Supporting Pension Systems**: An increased working-age population helps sustain public pension systems by expanding the tax base and reducing the dependency ratio. Migrants contribute to social security systems and help alleviate the financial pressures associated with an ageing population.

• **Economic and Social Balance**: Migration can help maintain economic balance by ensuring that there are enough workers to support various industries and services. This balance is crucial for maintaining social stability and preventing labour shortages that could otherwise impede economic growth.

In summary, migration has the potential to significantly benefit economies by filling labour gaps, contributing diverse skills and perspectives, and addressing demographic challenges. By understanding and leveraging these positive aspects of migration, countries can foster more inclusive and dynamic economies that harness the full potential of their migrant populations.

Chapter 3: Integration and Inclusion

Policy Frameworks

Effective integration of migrants into the economy and society requires comprehensive policy frameworks that address both economic and social aspects. Best practices in this area often include:

• **Inclusive Labour Market Policies**: Policies that promote equal access to employment opportunities for migrants are crucial. This includes recognizing foreign qualifications and providing pathways for skill recognition. Some countries have implemented credential recognition programs and partnerships with professional organisations to facilitate this process.

• **Legal Protections and Rights**: Ensuring that migrants have access to legal protections and labour rights is essential. This includes enforcing anti-discrimination laws, ensuring fair wages, and protecting against exploitative practices. Comprehensive labour laws and regulations help create a fair working environment for all employees, including migrants.

• **Social Welfare and Support Services**: Providing access to social services, including healthcare, housing, and legal assistance, supports the overall integration process. Policies that facilitate access to these services can help migrants settle more effectively and participate fully in the economy.

• **Community-Based Integration Programs**: Local integration initiatives, such as community centres and support networks, can play a significant role in helping migrants adjust to their new environments. These programs often provide essential information, resources, and social connections that facilitate integration.

• **Language and Cultural Training**: Offering language classes and cultural orientation programs can significantly improve migrants' ability to integrate into the local workforce and society. Language skills are particularly important for effective communication and access to various services.

Social Cohesion

Fostering social cohesion and reducing xenophobia are critical for creating inclusive societies where migrants can thrive. Strategies to achieve this include:

- **Promoting Diversity and Inclusion**: Public campaigns and educational programs that highlight the positive contributions of migrants and promote cultural understanding can help combat xenophobia. These initiatives often focus on celebrating cultural diversity and building bridges between different communities.

- **Engagement and Dialogue**: Encouraging dialogue and interaction between migrants and local communities helps build mutual understanding and reduce prejudice. Community events, cultural exchanges, and collaborative projects can facilitate positive interactions and strengthen social ties.

- **Anti-Discrimination Policies**: Implementing and enforcing anti-discrimination policies helps protect migrants from prejudice and ensures equal treatment in various aspects of life, including employment, housing, and education. Monitoring and addressing incidents of discrimination is essential for maintaining social cohesion.

- **Support for Social Networks**: Strengthening social networks and community support systems can help migrants build connections and integrate more effectively. Support groups, mentorship programs, and local organisations play a vital role in providing assistance and fostering a sense of belonging.

Educational and Training Programs

Enhancing the employability and skills of migrants through educational and training programs is a key component of successful integration:

• **Language and Vocational Training**: Language training programs are crucial for improving communication skills and increasing employability. Vocational training programs can provide migrants with specific skills and certifications relevant to local job markets. Tailoring these programs to the needs of different migrant groups helps ensure their effectiveness.

• **Accreditation and Recognition**: Programs that assist migrants in having their qualifications and experience recognized can facilitate their entry into professional fields. This includes processes for evaluating and validating foreign credentials and providing additional training if necessary.

• **Career Counseling and Job Placement Services**: Career counselling services can help migrants understand the local job market, develop effective resumes, and prepare for interviews. Job placement services can connect migrants with employment opportunities and provide support during the job search process.

• **Integration into Higher Education**: Providing pathways for migrants to access higher education and specialised training can enhance their career prospects. Support services for international students and scholarship opportunities can help address barriers to education and promote long-term success.

Successful integration and inclusion of migrants into the economy and society require a multifaceted approach that includes effective policy frameworks, strategies for fostering social cohesion, and targeted educational and training programs. By implementing best practices and addressing the challenges of integration, societies can create environments where migrants contribute fully and benefit from the opportunities available to them. This not only enhances economic growth but also strengthens social fabric and promotes a more inclusive and equitable society.

Chapter 4: The Dark Side: Exploitation of Workers

Types of Exploitation

Worker exploitation can manifest in various forms, each with significant implications for the well-being and rights of workers. Understanding these types is crucial for developing effective strategies to combat them.

- **Wage Theft**: Wage theft involves the illegal withholding of wages or benefits that workers are entitled to. This can include not paying the full amount owed, not paying overtime, or not providing promised benefits. Wage theft is a common issue among low-skilled and migrant workers who may lack the resources or knowledge to pursue legal action.

- **Poor Working Conditions**: Exploited workers often face unsafe and unhealthy working conditions. This can include exposure to hazardous materials, inadequate safety measures, excessive working hours, and lack of necessary breaks. Poor working conditions not only affect workers' health and safety but also contribute to broader public health issues.

- **Human Trafficking**: Human trafficking involves the coercion or deception of individuals into forced labour or commercial sexual exploitation. Victims of trafficking are often subjected to severe abuse, including physical violence, threats, and isolation. Migrant workers are particularly vulnerable to trafficking due to their precarious legal status and lack of social support.

- **Forced Labor and Debt Bondage**: Forced labour occurs when workers are compelled to work under threat or coercion, often with little to no pay. Debt bondage, a form of forced labour, involves workers being trapped in a cycle of debt that they can never repay, typically imposed by employers who exploit their desperate situations.

- **Exploitation of Migrant Workers**: Migrant workers can face exploitation due to their vulnerable status. This includes not only wage theft and poor working conditions but also being forced to work in jobs that do not match their skills or qualifications, and experiencing discrimination and harassment.

Vulnerable Populations

Certain groups are more susceptible to exploitation due to their specific circumstances and vulnerabilities:

- **Undocumented Migrants**: Undocumented migrants are at heightened risk of exploitation because of their lack of legal status. They may fear deportation and therefore tolerate abusive conditions without reporting violations. Their limited access to legal protections and social services further exacerbates their vulnerability.

- **Low-Skilled Workers**: Low-skilled workers, who often fill essential but undervalued roles, are particularly prone to exploitation. They may lack bargaining power, face limited job security, and be vulnerable to abusive practices due to their economic dependence on low-wage employment.

- **Seasonal and Temporary Workers**: Seasonal and temporary workers, who are often migrants, may face exploitation due to their transient status. Employers may take advantage of their temporary nature, offering low wages, poor working conditions, and limited job security.

- **Women and Minorities**: Women and minority groups can face additional layers of exploitation, including gender-based violence, lower wages, and discriminatory practices. Migrant women, in particular, may experience intersectional exploitation due to their gender, ethnicity, and immigration status.

Case Studies

- **Agricultural Sector in the United States**: In the U.S., migrant agricultural workers have faced significant exploitation issues, including wage theft, exposure to harmful chemicals, and poor living conditions. The notorious case of farmworker exploitation in California's Central Valley highlights systemic issues in the industry, despite efforts by advocacy groups to improve conditions.

- **Construction Industry in the Middle East**: Migrant workers in the construction industry in the Middle East have been subjected to severe exploitation, including forced labour, poor working conditions, and inadequate living arrangements. Reports from organisations like Human Rights Watch have documented widespread abuses in countries such as Qatar and the United Arab Emirates.

- **Garment Industry in Bangladesh**: The garment industry in Bangladesh has been plagued by poor working conditions and exploitation. The 2013 Rana Plaza disaster, where a garment factory collapsed killing over 1,100 workers, brought global attention to the dire conditions faced by workers in the sector. Issues such as low wages, long hours, and unsafe working environments are prevalent in the industry.

- **Domestic Work in Various Countries**: Domestic workers, including nannies, housekeepers, and caregivers, often face exploitation, particularly in informal employment settings. In many countries, domestic workers are excluded from labour protections and may experience low wages, long hours, and abusive conditions. High-profile cases, such as those reported by the International Labour Organization (ILO), have shed light on these issues.

The exploitation of workers, particularly migrants and low-skilled workers, represents a significant challenge that undermines human rights and economic fairness. Addressing these issues requires a multifaceted approach, including stronger legal protections, effective enforcement, and supportive measures for vulnerable populations. By understanding the various forms of exploitation and focusing on the most affected groups, societies can work towards creating fairer and more just labour markets for all workers.

Chapter 5: Legal and Regulatory Frameworks

Labour Laws

Labour laws play a crucial role in protecting workers, including migrants, from exploitation and ensuring fair treatment in the workplace. An examination of labour laws reveals several key areas of focus:

- **Employment Standards**: Many countries have established employment standards that cover minimum wages, working hours, overtime pay, and rest periods. These standards are designed to ensure fair compensation and working conditions for all workers, including migrants. For instance, the Fair Labor Standards Act (FLSA) in the United States sets minimum wage and overtime standards that apply to most workers.

- **Anti-Discrimination Laws**: Anti-discrimination laws aim to prevent discrimination based on race, nationality, gender, religion, and other characteristics. These laws are crucial for protecting migrant workers from unfair treatment and ensuring equal opportunities in employment. The Equality Act 2010 in the United Kingdom and the Civil Rights Act in the United States are examples of such legislation.

- **Health and Safety Regulations**: Occupational health and safety regulations are designed to protect workers from hazardous conditions and ensure safe working environments. These regulations often include requirements for workplace safety measures, training, and access to medical care. The Occupational Safety and Health Administration (OSHA) in the U.S. provides guidelines for workplace safety and health.

- **Work Permits and Visa Regulations**: Work permit and visa regulations govern the legal employment of migrants. These regulations define the terms under which migrants can work, including the types of jobs they can hold and the conditions of their employment. For example, the H-1B visa program in the U.S. allows skilled workers from abroad to work in specialised occupations.

Enforcement Challenges

Despite the existence of labour laws, enforcing these protections and addressing gaps in coverage can be challenging:

• **Lack of Enforcement Mechanisms**: In some countries, enforcement mechanisms for labour laws are weak or under-resourced. This can result in insufficient monitoring and inspections of workplaces, leaving gaps in the protection of workers. For example, limited labour inspection resources can make it difficult to identify and address violations.

• **Vulnerable Status of Migrants**: Migrant workers, particularly those who are undocumented or in temporary positions, may be reluctant to report labour violations due to fear of deportation or retaliation. This fear can hinder their access to justice and legal remedies.

• **Legal and Administrative Barriers**: Migrants may face legal and administrative barriers in accessing labour protections. This includes difficulties in navigating complex legal systems, language barriers, and lack of awareness about their rights. In some cases, the legal framework may not adequately address the specific needs and vulnerabilities of migrant workers.

• **Exploitation by Employers**: Employers may exploit gaps in labour laws or engage in practices that circumvent regulations. For example, some employers may use subcontracting arrangements to evade responsibilities, leaving workers without recourse.

International Standards

International standards and agreements play a critical role in shaping labour practices and protecting migrant workers globally:

• **International Labour Organization (ILO) Conventions**: The ILO, a specialised agency of the United Nations, has developed various conventions and recommendations related to migrant labour. Key conventions include:

○ **Convention No. 97 (Migration for Employment)**: Addresses the rights and conditions of migrant workers and promotes their integration into labour markets.

○ **Convention No. 143 (Migrant Workers)**: Focuses on the elimination of discriminatory practices against migrant workers and promotes fair treatment.

○ **Convention No. 181 (Private Employment Agencies)**: Regulates the activities of private employment agencies to ensure fair practices and protect workers from exploitation.

• **United Nations Global Compact for Safe, Orderly and Regular Migration**: This compact provides a framework for international cooperation on migration issues. It aims to improve migration governance, protect migrant rights, and enhance the benefits of migration for both migrants and host communities.

• **European Union Directives**: The European Union has developed several directives related to labour rights and migration, including the Directive on the Residence and Work Permit for Third-Country Nationals and the Directive on Seasonal Workers. These directives aim to harmonise labour standards and ensure fair treatment across member states.

• **Trade Agreements and Labor Standards**: Some international trade agreements include provisions related to labour standards and migrant rights. For example, trade agreements negotiated by the U.S. often include labour provisions that address worker protections and promote fair labour practices.

Legal and regulatory frameworks are essential for protecting migrant workers and ensuring fair labour practices. However, challenges in enforcement and gaps in protection can undermine these efforts. International standards and agreements provide valuable guidelines for improving labour protections and promoting fair treatment. By addressing enforcement challenges and strengthening legal frameworks, countries can work towards creating a more equitable and just labour environment for all workers.

Chapter 6: Addressing Exploitation

Advocacy and Reform

Non-governmental organisations (NGOs), advocacy groups, and reform initiatives play a crucial role in addressing and combating worker exploitation. Their efforts are often focused on raising awareness, influencing policy, and providing support to affected individuals:

- **Role of NGOs**: NGOs are instrumental in advocating for the rights of exploited workers and pushing for systemic changes. Organisations such as Human Rights Watch, Amnesty International, and the International Labor Rights Forum work to highlight abuses, provide support to victims, and lobby for stronger protections. They often conduct research, publish reports, and engage in public awareness campaigns to bring attention to exploitation issues.

- **Advocacy Groups**: Advocacy groups, including labour unions and worker rights organisations, work to improve conditions for workers through lobbying, policy recommendations, and grassroots mobilisation. For example, the International Trade Union Confederation (ITUC) represents workers globally and advocates for fair labour standards and protections.

- **Reform Initiatives**: Reform initiatives often focus on legislative changes and policy improvements. This includes efforts to strengthen labour laws, enhance enforcement mechanisms, and address gaps in protections. Successful reform initiatives can lead to significant improvements in worker rights and conditions, as seen in various countries that have implemented comprehensive labour reforms.

Corporate Responsibility

Businesses have a critical role to play in ensuring fair labour practices and maintaining ethical supply chains. Corporate responsibility involves:

- **Ethical Supply Chains**: Companies are increasingly expected to ensure that their supply chains adhere to ethical labour practices. This includes conducting regular audits, implementing fair labour standards, and addressing any issues of exploitation or abuse. Organisations like the Ethical Trading Initiative (ETI) and the Fair Trade Foundation provide frameworks and certifications to guide companies in maintaining ethical supply chains.

- **Corporate Social Responsibility (CSR)**: CSR programs often focus on improving labour conditions and supporting community development. Companies with robust CSR initiatives may engage in partnerships with NGOs, support fair trade practices, and invest in projects that promote worker well-being and rights.

- **Transparency and Accountability**: Transparency in business practices is essential for addressing exploitation. Companies are encouraged to publish reports on their labour practices, supply chain management, and efforts to combat exploitation. Accountability mechanisms, such as grievance systems and third-party audits, help ensure that companies uphold their commitments to ethical practices.

- **Employee Training and Support**: Businesses can provide training for employees on labour rights, anti-exploitation measures, and reporting mechanisms. Additionally, support for workers, including access to legal assistance and counselling, can help address issues of exploitation and ensure fair treatment.

Government Initiatives

Effective government policies and programs are crucial for preventing and addressing worker exploitation. Key government initiatives include:

- **Strengthening Labour Laws**: Governments can enhance labour laws to provide better protections for workers, including stronger regulations on wages, working conditions, and occupational health and safety. This may involve updating existing laws, closing loopholes, and implementing new regulations to address emerging issues.

- **Enforcement and Inspections**: Increasing resources for labour inspections and enforcement is essential for identifying and addressing exploitation. Governments can strengthen enforcement mechanisms by expanding inspection programs, improving coordination among agencies, and ensuring that violations are addressed promptly and effectively.

- **Support Services for Victims**: Governments can provide support services for victims of exploitation, including access to legal assistance, counselling, and emergency relief. Specialised services for migrant workers and other vulnerable populations can help them navigate legal processes and access necessary support.

- **International Cooperation**: Addressing exploitation often requires international cooperation and coordination. Governments can participate in international agreements and initiatives aimed at improving labour standards and combating exploitation. Collaborative efforts with other countries and international organisations can enhance the effectiveness of anti-exploitation measures.

- **Public Awareness and Education**: Government initiatives that promote public awareness and education about labour rights and exploitation can help prevent abuses and empower workers. Educational campaigns, training programs, and informational resources can raise awareness and promote a culture of respect for worker rights.

Addressing exploitation requires a multifaceted approach involving advocacy and reform, corporate responsibility, and effective government initiatives. NGOs and advocacy groups play a critical role in highlighting abuses and pushing for systemic changes, while businesses are increasingly held accountable for ethical practices and supply chain management. Governments must strengthen labour laws, enhance enforcement, and provide support for victims to create a fair and just labour environment. By combining efforts across these areas, societies can work towards eradicating exploitation and ensuring that all workers are treated with dignity and respect.

Chapter 7: Balancing Growth and Protection

Policy Recommendations

Balancing economic growth with the protection of migrant workers involves implementing strategies that promote both economic benefits and fair labour practices. Key policy recommendations include:

- **Integrated Migration and Labor Policies**: Develop comprehensive migration policies that align with labour market needs while ensuring protections for migrants. This includes creating pathways for legal migration that match labour demands and providing mechanisms for regularising the status of undocumented workers.

- **Enhanced Labor Standards and Protections**: Strengthen labour standards to ensure that migrant workers receive fair treatment. This includes enforcing minimum wage laws, occupational health and safety standards, and anti-discrimination protections. Policies should also address wage theft and exploitative practices specific to migrant workers.

- **Collaborative Frameworks**: Foster collaboration between governments, businesses, and civil society organisations to address migration and labour issues. Public-private partnerships can help develop effective integration programs, improve monitoring and enforcement, and promote ethical business practices.

- **Support for Migrant Integration**: Implement policies that support the social and economic integration of migrants, such as language and vocational training programs, access to education, and community support services. These measures can enhance migrants' employability and social cohesion.

- **Regular Monitoring and Evaluation**: Establish mechanisms for monitoring and evaluating the impact of migration and labour policies.

Regular assessments can help identify gaps in protections, measure the effectiveness of policies, and make necessary adjustments to balance growth with worker protections.

Best Practices

Successful integration and protection strategies from around the world offer valuable lessons for balancing economic growth and worker protection:

- **Germany's Integration Policies**: Germany has implemented comprehensive integration programs for migrants, including language courses, job placement services, and educational opportunities. The country's approach combines economic needs with strong support systems, resulting in successful labour market integration and social cohesion.

- **Canada's Express Entry System**: Canada's Express Entry system selects skilled migrants based on labour market needs and provides pathways for permanent residency. This system balances economic growth with protection by ensuring that migrants contribute to the economy while receiving legal rights and protections.

- **New Zealand's Employment Standards**: New Zealand has strong labour laws that include protections for all workers, regardless of their migration status. The country's emphasis on fair wages, safe working conditions, and anti-discrimination measures helps protect migrant workers while fostering economic growth.

- **Sweden's Inclusive Approach**: Sweden has developed policies that focus on both economic integration and social inclusion. This includes support for migrant entrepreneurship, access to education, and anti-discrimination measures. Sweden's approach has led to successful integration outcomes and a positive impact on the economy.

Future Trends

Emerging trends in migration and labour markets are likely to shape the future of growth and protection strategies:

- **Digital Transformation and Remote Work**: The rise of digital technologies and remote work is changing labour market dynamics. Migrant workers may increasingly have opportunities to engage in remote and digital economies, which can offer more flexibility and better working conditions. However, this trend also raises questions about labour rights and protections in virtual work environments.

- **Increased Migration Flows**: Global migration is expected to continue increasing due to factors such as economic disparities, climate change, and geopolitical conflicts. Policymakers will need to adapt strategies to manage growing migration flows while ensuring that protections and integration measures remain effective.

- **Focus on Human Rights and Ethical Labour Practices**: There is a growing emphasis on human rights and ethical labour practices globally. Businesses and governments are increasingly expected to uphold labour rights and implement fair practices. This trend may lead to more stringent regulations and greater accountability for exploitation.

- **Technological Innovations in Monitoring and Enforcement**: Advances in technology, such as data analytics and artificial intelligence, may enhance the ability to monitor labour practices and enforce regulations. These tools can help identify exploitation and improve compliance with labour standards.

- **Shifts in Global Labor Markets**: Changes in global labour markets, including shifts in industry demands and job automation, will impact migration patterns and worker protections. Adapting policies to address these shifts will be crucial for balancing economic growth with the protection of workers.

Balancing economic growth with the protection of migrant workers requires a multifaceted approach that includes effective policy recommendations, adoption of best practices, and adaptation to emerging trends. By developing integrated migration and labour policies, fostering collaboration, and learning from successful strategies, societies can achieve both economic benefits and fair treatment for migrant workers. Staying informed about future trends and adapting policies accordingly will be essential for maintaining this balance and ensuring that growth and protection go hand in hand.

Conclusion

Summary of Key Points

Migration presents both significant economic benefits and serious challenges that must be addressed to create a fair and just labour environment. Key points covered in this book include:

1. **Economic Benefits of Migration**: Migration drives economic growth through labour market contributions, innovation, and entrepreneurship. Migrants help fill labour gaps, contribute diverse skills and perspectives, and address demographic challenges such as population decline and ageing populations. Case studies from various countries and sectors illustrate how migrants positively impact economies and foster growth.

2. **Positive Migration Economy**: Migrants play a crucial role in enhancing labour market dynamics, driving innovation, and offering demographic benefits. Their contributions to productivity and economic development are vital for addressing labour shortages and supporting economic expansion.

3. **Integration and Inclusion**: Effective integration strategies, including comprehensive policy frameworks, social cohesion efforts, and educational and training programs, are essential for successfully integrating migrants into the economy and society. These strategies help promote social inclusion and reduce xenophobia.

4. **Exploitation of Workers**: Despite the benefits of migration, worker exploitation remains a significant issue. Forms of exploitation include wage theft, poor working conditions, human trafficking, and forced labour. Vulnerable populations

such as undocumented migrants and low-skilled workers face heightened risks. Case studies highlight the severe impact of exploitation in various industries and regions.

5. **Legal and Regulatory Frameworks**: Strong labour laws, effective enforcement, and international standards are crucial for protecting migrant workers. Challenges in enforcement and gaps in protection often undermine these efforts. International agreements and standards provide important guidelines for improving labour practices and protecting workers' rights.

6. **Addressing Exploitation**: Combating exploitation requires coordinated efforts from NGOs, advocacy groups, businesses, and governments. Effective strategies include advocacy and reform initiatives, corporate responsibility, and government policies. Successful examples from around the world demonstrate the potential for positive change when these approaches are implemented.

7. **Balancing Growth and Protection**: Balancing economic growth with worker protection involves integrating migration and labour policies, adopting best practices, and adapting to emerging trends. Future trends, such as digital transformation and increased migration flows, will shape the landscape of migration and labour markets.

Call to Action

To ensure that migration continues to be a force for positive economic growth while addressing the challenges of worker exploitation, it is essential for all stakeholders to take proactive steps:

- **Governments**: Develop and implement comprehensive migration and labour policies that balance economic needs with worker protections. Strengthen enforcement mechanisms, provide support services for vulnerable populations, and foster international cooperation to address global migration challenges.

• **Businesses**: Commit to ethical labour practices and ensure that supply chains are free from exploitation. Embrace corporate social responsibility and transparency, and support fair labour practices throughout operations.

• **NGOs and Advocacy Groups**: Continue to advocate for the rights of migrants and work towards systemic reforms. Raise awareness about exploitation, provide support to affected individuals, and collaborate with policymakers and businesses to drive positive change.

• **Communities and Individuals**: Promote social inclusion and support policies that foster fair treatment of migrants. Educate others about migration and labour rights, and advocate for practices that protect all workers from exploitation.

By working together towards fair and sustainable migration practices, we can harness the economic benefits of migration while ensuring that all workers are treated with dignity and respect. The future of migration and labour markets depends on our collective efforts to create a more equitable and just world.

Migration and Wealth Management: The Impact of Wall Street on Global Mobility

Introduction

Migration has long been a fundamental aspect of human history, driven by the quest for better opportunities, safety, and quality of life. In recent decades, however, the intersection of migration and wealth management has become increasingly pronounced. This book aims to explore how modern migration patterns are shaped by sophisticated wealth management strategies and how Wall Street and the broader financial markets influence global mobility.

Wealth management encompasses a range of financial services designed to help individuals and families grow, preserve, and transfer their wealth. It includes investment strategies, tax planning, estate planning, and more. For high-net-worth individuals and families, migration is not just about finding a new place to live; it's often a strategic decision influenced by financial goals and opportunities. This book will delve into how these wealth management strategies impact migration decisions and how global financial markets play a crucial role in this dynamic.

Overview

In this book, we will explore the complex relationship between migration, wealth management, and financial markets. We will begin by examining the fundamental drivers of migration, including historical trends and modern patterns. Understanding these factors will provide a foundation for analysing how wealth management practices intersect with migration decisions.

We will then delve into the role of Wall Street and the stock markets in shaping migration trends. The stock market's fluctuations, economic conditions, and investment opportunities can significantly influence migration decisions, particularly for those with substantial financial resources. By examining these influences, we will gain insight into how financial markets drive global mobility.

The book will also cover various aspects of wealth management that impact migration, including investment opportunities abroad, tax optimization, and wealth preservation strategies. Through case studies and real-life examples, we will illustrate how individuals and families have strategically managed their wealth to facilitate migration and secure their financial futures.

Additionally, we will address the broader economic and social implications of migration, both for host and home countries. The effects on labour markets, public services, and global economic trends will be explored to understand the ripple effects of migration driven by financial considerations.

We will also navigate the regulatory and legal landscape affecting migration and wealth management, highlighting the challenges and solutions for navigating complex immigration policies and financial regulations.

Emerging trends, such as technological advancements and the impact of climate change, will be discussed to provide a forward-looking perspective on migration and wealth management.

Through a combination of historical context, contemporary analysis, and future projections, this book aims to offer a comprehensive understanding of how wealth management and financial markets shape global migration patterns. By bridging these interconnected domains, we hope to illuminate the strategic considerations behind migration decisions and the broader implications for individuals and societies alike.

Chapter 1: The Dynamics of Migration

Historical Perspectives

Migration has been a defining feature of human civilization, with patterns evolving through various historical epochs. Early migrations were often driven by the search for arable land, resources, and trade opportunities. For instance, the Great Migrations of the early mediaeval period involved the movement of various groups across Europe and Asia, shaping the geopolitical landscape of the time.

The Age of Exploration (15th to 17th centuries) marked a significant shift, as European powers ventured across oceans, leading to the colonisation of the Americas, Africa, and parts of Asia. This period was characterized by both voluntary migrations, driven by the pursuit of wealth and land, and forced migrations, such as the transatlantic slave trade.

In the 19th and early 20th centuries, migration patterns were influenced by industrialization and urbanisation. The Industrial Revolution prompted large-scale movements from rural areas to cities in search of employment, while global migration was also driven by economic opportunities in the Americas, Australia, and other parts of the world.

The aftermath of World War II saw a new era of migration, with significant movements driven by decolonization, economic reconstruction, and the search for better living conditions. The late 20th and early 21st centuries have continued to see significant migration driven by economic globalisation, regional conflicts, and technological advancements.

Modern Migration Patterns

In contemporary times, migration patterns are characterised by increased complexity and diversity. Key trends include:

- **Economic Migration**: Individuals and families moving to countries with stronger economies and better job opportunities. This includes both skilled professionals seeking high-paying jobs and low-skilled workers looking for better wages and living conditions.

- **Refugee Movements**: Driven by conflicts, persecution, and instability, millions of people are forced to flee their home countries. The Syrian civil war, for instance, led to a massive refugee crisis, with millions seeking asylum in Europe and neighbouring countries.

- **Skilled Labor Migration**: High-demand sectors such as technology, healthcare, and engineering attract skilled workers from around the world. Countries with robust innovation hubs and technological sectors, like the United States and Germany, are popular destinations for skilled migrants.

- **International Student Migration**: Education remains a significant driver of migration, with students moving to pursue higher education in countries known for their prestigious institutions and research opportunities.

- **Retirement Migration**: Increasingly, retirees are choosing to relocate to countries with favourable climates, lower living costs, and attractive retirement benefits.

Factors Driving Migration

Several key factors influence modern migration patterns:

- **Economic Opportunities**: The pursuit of better employment prospects, higher wages, and improved living standards are primary motivators for economic migration. Regions experiencing economic growth and job creation attract workers from less prosperous areas.

- **Political Instability**: Wars, conflicts, and political repression drive large-scale refugee movements. Political instability can create environments of violence and persecution, compelling individuals and families to seek safety elsewhere.

- **Environmental Factors**: Climate change, natural disasters, and environmental degradation are increasingly affecting migration patterns. Rising sea levels, extreme weather events, and resource scarcity can displace communities and drive migration to more stable regions.

- **Social Influences**: Social factors, including family reunification, cultural connections, and established immigrant communities, play a significant role in migration decisions. Individuals may move to join relatives or communities where they have social ties and cultural familiarity.

- **Legal and Policy Frameworks**: Immigration policies, visa regulations, and international agreements shape migration flows. Policies that facilitate or restrict movement can significantly impact patterns of migration.

- **Technological Advancements**: Advances in communication and transportation technologies make it easier for people to move and maintain connections with their home countries. Digital platforms also provide information and resources that influence migration decisions.

By understanding these historical and contemporary migration trends, as well as the driving factors behind them, we can better grasp how wealth management strategies and financial markets impact global mobility. This foundational knowledge sets the stage for exploring the intricate relationships between migration, wealth management, and financial systems in the subsequent chapters.

Chapter 2: Wealth Management and Migration

Definition and Importance of Wealth Management

Wealth management is a comprehensive service that involves financial planning, investment management, and other strategies aimed at preserving and growing an individual's or family's wealth. It is particularly relevant for high-net-worth individuals (HNWIs) and families who have substantial financial assets and complex financial needs. Key components of wealth management include:

● **Financial Planning**: This involves creating a long-term strategy for managing an individual's or family's finances, including budgeting, retirement planning, and estate planning. Financial planning ensures that resources are allocated efficiently to meet both short-term and long-term goals.

● **Investment Strategies**: Wealth management includes developing and implementing investment strategies to grow assets. This may involve a diversified portfolio of stocks, bonds, real estate, and alternative investments tailored to the client's risk tolerance, time horizon, and financial objectives.

● **Asset Protection**: Protecting wealth from potential risks, including legal disputes, economic downturns, and fraud, is a crucial aspect of wealth management. This may involve setting up trusts, insurance policies, and other mechanisms to safeguard assets.

● **Tax Optimization**: Efficient tax planning is essential to minimise tax liabilities and maximise after-tax returns. Wealth managers work to implement strategies that reduce taxes on income, investments, and estates.

- **Estate Planning**: Preparing for the transfer of assets upon death involves estate planning strategies such as wills, trusts, and charitable giving. Effective estate planning ensures that wealth is passed on according to the client's wishes while minimising tax implications.
- **Philanthropy**: Many HNWIs and families engage in philanthropic activities. Wealth management includes planning charitable donations and setting up foundations or donor-advised funds to achieve philanthropic goals.

Role of Wealth Management in Migration

Wealth management plays a significant role in migration, particularly for those with substantial financial resources. Key aspects include:

- **Facilitating Relocation**: Wealth management strategies can ease the process of relocating to a new country. This includes managing the sale or purchase of real estate, transferring assets, and ensuring financial stability during the transition.
- **Tax Considerations**: High-net-worth individuals often seek to optimise their tax situations when moving to a new country. Wealth managers help navigate the tax implications of immigration, including understanding the tax treaties between countries and structuring investments to minimise tax liabilities.
- **Investment Opportunities**: Wealthy individuals may relocate to take advantage of investment opportunities in new markets. This includes investing in local businesses, real estate, or emerging markets with high growth potential.
- **Legal and Regulatory Compliance**: Migration involves navigating various legal and regulatory requirements. Wealth managers assist with ensuring compliance with immigration laws, asset reporting requirements, and financial regulations in the new country.
- **Lifestyle and Security**: Wealth management also addresses personal lifestyle preferences and security concerns. This includes finding suitable residential properties, establishing relationships with

local financial advisors, and ensuring personal safety and security in the new environment.

- **Education and Healthcare**: For families, relocating often involves considerations for education and healthcare. Wealth managers assist in finding high-quality educational institutions and healthcare services, and managing related expenses.

Case Studies

1. The Smith Family: Relocating for Tax Optimization

○ **Background**: The Smith family, a wealthy couple with significant investments and a successful business, sought to relocate from the United States to Switzerland.

○ **Motivation**: They were motivated by Switzerland's favourable tax regime, which offered significant tax savings compared to their home country.

○ **Wealth Management Strategy**: Their wealth manager facilitated the sale of their U.S. properties, advised on Swiss tax laws, and helped transfer their investments to Switzerland while minimising tax liabilities.

○ **Outcome**: The Smiths successfully relocated, benefiting from tax optimization and new investment opportunities in Switzerland's financial market.

2. Dr. Li: Moving for Investment Opportunities

○ **Background**: Dr. Li, a renowned scientist from China, decided to move to the United States to join a leading research institution.

○ **Motivation**: The move provided access to advanced research facilities and potential investment in biotech startups.

○ **Wealth Management Strategy**: Dr. Li's wealth manager coordinated the transfer of her assets, set up a diversified investment portfolio including biotech stocks, and advised on real estate investments in the U.S.

○ **Outcome**: Dr. Li successfully integrated into her new role and made significant investments in biotech, enhancing her professional and financial standing.

3. The Patel Family: Seeking a Better Quality of Life

○ **Background**: The Patel family from India decided to relocate to Canada to offer their children better educational opportunities and a higher quality of life.

○ **Motivation**: They were attracted by Canada's high-quality education system and stable political environment.

○ **Wealth Management Strategy**: Their wealth manager helped with the purchase of a home in a desirable location, set up education funds for their children, and ensured compliance with Canadian immigration and tax regulations.

○ **Outcome**: The Patel family settled comfortably in Canada, with their children attending top schools and their financial needs well-managed.

These case studies illustrate how wealth management strategies facilitate migration for various reasons, from optimising tax situations to pursuing investment opportunities and enhancing lifestyle quality. Understanding these real-life examples provides valuable insights into the practical application of wealth management in the context of global mobility.

Chapter 3: Wall Street and Global Migration

Overview of Wall Street

Wall Street, located in the Financial District of Manhattan, New York City, is a global hub for financial markets and services. It is home to some of the most significant financial institutions, including major investment banks, stock exchanges, and brokerage firms. Wall Street's influence extends far beyond its geographical location, impacting global finance and investment through its extensive network of financial markets and institutions.

Key components of Wall Street include:

• **Stock Exchanges**: The New York Stock Exchange (NYSE) and NASDAQ are two of the largest and most influential stock exchanges globally. They facilitate the trading of securities and are central to the functioning of financial markets.

• **Investment Banks**: Major investment banks, such as Goldman Sachs, JPMorgan Chase, and Morgan Stanley, provide services including underwriting, advisory, and trading. These institutions play a crucial role in capital markets and financial transactions.

• **Brokerage Firms**: Firms that buy and sell securities on behalf of clients. They provide access to financial markets for individual and institutional investors.

• **Asset Management Companies**: These firms manage investments on behalf of clients, including mutual funds, hedge funds, and private equity. They play a key role in wealth management and investment strategies.

• **Financial Regulators**: Institutions such as the Securities and Exchange Commission (SEC) oversee financial markets and enforce regulations to ensure transparency and protect investors.

Wall Street's global influence stems from its role in capital allocation, risk management, and financial innovation. The decisions made on Wall Street affect global financial markets, economies, and, consequently, migration patterns.

Stock Market Influences on Migration

Stock market fluctuations and overall economic conditions have a significant impact on migration decisions. Here's how:

- **Economic Conditions**: Economic booms or downturns influence migration trends. During periods of economic prosperity, individuals and families may be more inclined to move to countries or cities with growing job opportunities and higher living standards. Conversely, economic downturns or financial crises can lead to increased migration as individuals seek stability and better prospects elsewhere.

- **Investment Opportunities**: High-net-worth individuals and investors often move to capitalise on lucrative investment opportunities. For example, a booming tech sector in a particular city may attract skilled professionals and investors seeking to benefit from the growth potential of that sector. Similarly, countries with emerging markets or favourable investment climates may see an influx of investors looking to diversify their portfolios.

- **Financial Market Volatility**: Significant fluctuations in financial markets can prompt migration as individuals and businesses seek safer or more stable environments. For instance, political instability or financial crises in one country may drive wealthy individuals to relocate to countries with more stable financial systems.

- **Currency Fluctuations**: Changes in currency values can impact migration decisions. A strong currency in one country may attract international investors and expatriates, while a weak currency might push individuals and businesses to seek opportunities in more economically stable regions.

Financial Markets and Migration Trends

The influence of financial markets on migration trends is evident in various ways:

- **Relocation of Financial Services Professionals**: Financial market developments often lead to the relocation of finance professionals. For instance, global financial hubs such as New York, London, and Hong Kong attract talent from around the world due to their central role in global finance. Changes in regulations, market opportunities, or financial crises can also lead to shifts in these hubs, impacting where professionals choose to live and work.

- **Investment Migration**: Investment migration programs, such as citizenship or residency-by-investment schemes, allow individuals to obtain residency or citizenship in a new country through significant financial investments. These programs are often influenced by global financial trends and market conditions, attracting wealthy individuals seeking new opportunities or a better quality of life.

- **Impact of Financial Innovation**: Innovations in financial markets, such as the rise of fintech and blockchain technologies, can create new migration trends. For example, cities known for their fintech ecosystems may attract entrepreneurs and professionals from around the world, leading to shifts in migration patterns based on emerging financial technologies.

- **Global Talent Mobility**: As financial markets become increasingly interconnected, there is greater mobility of talent across borders. Financial institutions may relocate operations or open new offices in response to market demands, leading to the movement of employees and their families to new locations.

- **Economic Zones and Special Investment Areas**: Countries and regions with special economic zones or investment incentives can attract foreign investors and professionals. Financial markets influence the attractiveness of these zones, impacting migration patterns as individuals and businesses move to capitalise on favourable conditions.

Through the lens of Wall Street and global financial markets, we can observe how financial dynamics shape migration patterns. Understanding these influences helps illuminate the strategic decisions behind migration and the broader implications for individuals and economies.

Chapter 4: Investment Strategies and Migration

Investment Opportunities Abroad

Investment opportunities abroad often drive migration, particularly for high-net-worth individuals and businesses seeking to capitalise on new markets or favourable conditions. Key types of investment opportunities that influence migration include:

• **Real Estate**: Investing in real estate is a common motivation for migration. Individuals and families may move to countries with robust real estate markets, offering potential for high returns on investment. Real estate investments can include residential properties, commercial real estate, and vacation homes. Cities with growing real estate markets or attractive property prices often draw investors looking to diversify their portfolios.

• **Business Ventures**: Opportunities to invest in or start new businesses abroad can drive migration. Entrepreneurs may relocate to countries with favourable business climates, access to emerging markets, or supportive regulatory environments. This includes investing in startups, acquiring existing businesses, or entering new industry sectors.

• **Tax Havens**: Some individuals and businesses move to countries with favourable tax regimes or low tax rates. Tax havens offer opportunities for significant tax savings through lower corporate taxes, income taxes, and estate taxes. Migration to these jurisdictions is often driven by the desire to optimise tax liabilities and preserve wealth.

• **Financial Markets**: Access to advanced financial markets and investment opportunities can attract international investors. Countries with well-developed financial systems, stock exchanges, and investment infrastructure offer opportunities for high returns and strategic financial planning.

• **Emerging Markets**: Investors may seek opportunities in emerging markets with high growth potential. Migration to these regions allows individuals and businesses to capitalise on rapidly developing economies, expanding consumer bases, and innovative industries.

• **Residency and Citizenship-by-Investment Programs**: Some countries offer residency or citizenship through significant financial investments. These programs provide investors with access to new markets, improved quality of life, and enhanced mobility, often in exchange for substantial financial contributions.

Tax Optimization and Wealth Preservation

Tax laws and wealth preservation strategies are crucial considerations in migration decisions. Effective tax planning and asset protection can significantly influence where individuals and businesses choose to relocate. Key factors include:

• **Tax Laws and Regulations**: Different countries have varying tax laws affecting income, investments, and estates. Individuals and businesses may migrate to jurisdictions with favourable tax laws to reduce tax liabilities. This can include lower personal income taxes, reduced corporate tax rates, or favourable treatment of capital gains.

• **Tax Treaties**: International tax treaties can impact migration decisions by reducing the risk of double taxation. Tax treaties between countries often provide relief for individuals and businesses operating in multiple jurisdictions, making certain locations more attractive for migration.

• **Wealth Preservation Strategies**: Protecting wealth from potential risks such as political instability, economic downturns, or legal disputes is a key aspect of wealth management. Strategies such as setting up trusts, establishing offshore accounts, and diversifying investments can influence migration decisions.

- **Estate Planning**: Estate planning involves arranging the transfer of assets upon death to minimise taxes and ensure that wealth is passed on according to one's wishes. Individuals may relocate to countries with favourable estate tax laws or more flexible estate planning options.

- **Asset Protection**: Asset protection involves safeguarding assets from potential claims, creditors, or legal disputes. Migration to jurisdictions with strong asset protection laws can be a strategic decision for preserving wealth and ensuring financial security.

Case Studies

1. The Johnsons: Real Estate Investment and Migration

- **Background**: The Johnson family, high-net-worth individuals from the United Kingdom, sought to relocate to Portugal to take advantage of the booming real estate market and favourable tax incentives.

- **Motivation**: Portugal's attractive property prices, along with the Golden Visa program offering residency through real estate investment, were key factors in their decision.

- **Investment Strategy**: They purchased multiple properties in Lisbon and Porto, focusing on rental income and long-term capital appreciation. The family also benefited from Portugal's favourable tax regime for expatriates.

- **Outcome**: The Johnsons successfully established themselves in Portugal, enjoying both lucrative real estate investments and a favourable tax environment.

2. The Chen Family: Business Ventures and Migration

○ **Background**: The Chen family, successful entrepreneurs from China, moved to Singapore to expand their technology business.

○ **Motivation**: Singapore's business-friendly environment, robust financial infrastructure, and strategic location in Asia made it an attractive destination for their expansion.

○ **Investment Strategy**: They set up a new office in Singapore, taking advantage of the city's vibrant tech sector and supportive government policies. The Chens also invested in local startups and real estate.

○ **Outcome**: The family's business thrived in Singapore, and they benefited from the country's strong economic growth and investor-friendly climate.

3. The Rodriguez Family: Tax Optimization and Relocation

○ **Background**: The Rodriguez family, originally from Argentina, moved to the Cayman Islands to optimise their tax situation and protect their wealth.

○ **Motivation**: The Cayman Islands' reputation as a tax haven, with no direct taxes on income or capital gains, was a significant factor in their decision.

○ **Investment Strategy**: They restructured their investment portfolio, establishing offshore accounts and trusts to maximise tax efficiency. The family also acquired property in the Cayman Islands.

○ **Outcome**: The Rodriguezes achieved substantial tax savings and enhanced their wealth preservation strategies, while enjoying a favourable living environment.

These case studies illustrate how various investment strategies and tax considerations drive migration decisions for high-net-worth individuals and businesses. Understanding these dynamics provides valuable insights into the interplay between investment opportunities, tax optimization, and global mobility.

Chapter 5: Economic and Social Implications of Migration

Impact on Host Countries

Migration has a profound effect on the economies and societies of host countries. These impacts can be both positive and negative, and they often vary depending on the scale of migration and the specific context of the host country.

- **Labour Markets**: Migrants often fill labour shortages in various sectors, from high-skilled professions to low-skilled jobs. This can boost economic productivity and growth. For example, skilled migrants in technology or healthcare can drive innovation and fill critical gaps in these industries. However, an influx of low-skilled migrants might lead to increased competition for jobs, potentially impacting wages and employment opportunities for local workers.

- **Public Services**: The arrival of migrants can place additional demands on public services, such as education, healthcare, and social welfare systems. This can strain resources, particularly in regions with large numbers of migrants. However, migrants also contribute to public services through taxes and social contributions, which can help offset some of these costs.

- **Economic Growth**: Migrants often contribute to economic growth by increasing consumer demand and entrepreneurship. They create new businesses, invest in local economies, and contribute to the expansion of markets. Additionally, diverse workforces can enhance innovation and creativity.

- **Cultural and Social Dynamics**: Migration brings cultural diversity and can enrich the social fabric of host countries. It fosters multiculturalism and promotes cultural exchange. However, it can also lead to social tensions and challenges related to integration and cohesion, particularly if there are significant cultural or linguistic differences.

- **Housing and Infrastructure**: Increased migration can impact housing markets and infrastructure. In high-demand areas, this can lead to higher property prices and rents, potentially affecting affordability for local residents. Infrastructure, including transportation and public amenities, may also need to be expanded to accommodate growing populations.

Impact on Home Countries

Migration also has significant implications for home countries, affecting their economies and social structures in various ways.

- **Brain Drain**: The departure of highly skilled professionals and talented individuals, known as brain drain, can weaken the home country's workforce and impede economic development. This loss of talent can hinder innovation, productivity, and overall growth in sectors that are critical for the home country's development.

- **Remittances**: Migrants often send money back to their home countries, providing a crucial source of income for many families. Remittances can boost local economies, improve living standards, and fund education and healthcare. They can also help stabilise economies by providing a steady flow of foreign currency.

- **Social Impacts**: Migration can affect family structures and social dynamics in home countries. The absence of working-age adults might impact household dynamics and community structures. Additionally, migration can influence cultural exchanges and shift social attitudes within home countries.

- **Economic Opportunities**: Migration can create new economic opportunities in home countries through the establishment of transnational businesses and investments. Return migrants may bring back skills, knowledge, and capital that can benefit their home countries' economies.

Global Economic Trends

Global economic trends, influenced by financial markets and international economic policies, have a significant impact on migration patterns and wealth management.

- **Economic Cycles**: Global economic booms and downturns affect migration patterns. Economic growth can drive migration to countries with expanding job markets and investment opportunities. Conversely, economic recessions can prompt migration as individuals and businesses seek stability and new opportunities.

- **Financial Market Volatility**: Fluctuations in financial markets can influence migration decisions. Economic instability or financial crises in one region can lead to increased migration as people seek safer and more stable environments. Conversely, robust financial markets and investment climates can attract skilled professionals and investors.

- **Globalisation**: The process of globalisation has increased economic interdependence and mobility. Improved transportation and communication technologies facilitate international migration, enabling individuals and businesses to operate across borders more easily.

- **Economic Policies**: International trade agreements, economic policies, and financial regulations shape migration trends. Policies that promote economic openness and investment can attract migrants seeking opportunities in dynamic economies. Conversely, restrictive trade policies and protectionism can impact migration by limiting economic growth and opportunities.

- **Technological Advancements**: Advances in technology, including digital finance and remote work, influence migration patterns. Technology enables global connectivity and allows individuals to work from various locations, impacting migration decisions related to lifestyle and career opportunities.

- **Climate Change**: Emerging trends related to climate change and environmental sustainability are also shaping migration patterns.

Rising sea levels, extreme weather events, and resource scarcity can drive migration as individuals and communities seek safer and more sustainable living conditions.

By examining these economic and social implications of migration, we gain a deeper understanding of how migration affects both host and home countries. These insights highlight the complex interplay between migration, wealth management, and global economic trends, providing a comprehensive perspective on the multifaceted impacts of migration.

Chapter 6: Regulatory and Legal Considerations

Immigration Policies

Immigration policies are crucial in shaping migration patterns and influence various aspects of wealth management. They encompass rules and regulations that govern the entry, stay, and status of individuals in a foreign country. Understanding these policies is essential for both migrants and wealth managers.

- **Types of Immigration Policies**: Immigration policies vary widely by country and may include:

  - **Visa Requirements**: Countries have specific visa categories for different purposes, such as work, study, investment, and tourism. These requirements dictate the terms under which individuals can enter and stay in the country.

  - **Residency Permits**: Long-term residency permits allow individuals to live and work in a country for extended periods. These permits often have specific requirements related to income, employment, or investment.

  - **Citizenship-by-Investment**: Some countries offer pathways to citizenship through significant financial investments. These programs typically require substantial investments in real estate, government bonds, or business ventures.

  - **Asylum and Refugee Policies**: Countries have procedures for granting asylum or refugee status to individuals fleeing persecution or conflict. These policies include criteria for eligibility and processes for application and review.

• **Impact on Migration**: Immigration policies influence the ease or difficulty of relocating to a new country. Stringent policies may deter potential migrants, while more flexible or favourable policies can attract skilled professionals, investors, and entrepreneurs.

• **Impact on Wealth Management**: Immigration policies affect how wealth is managed across borders. For example, policies related to residency and citizenship can impact tax liabilities, investment opportunities, and estate planning. Wealth managers must navigate these policies to provide effective advice and solutions for their clients.

Financial Regulations

Financial regulations and compliance requirements are essential for managing wealth internationally. They govern how financial transactions, investments, and asset management are conducted across borders.

• **Anti-Money Laundering (AML) and Know Your Customer (KYC) Regulations**: Financial institutions are required to adhere to AML and KYC regulations to prevent money laundering and ensure that clients are properly vetted. These regulations impact international transactions and investments, requiring thorough documentation and compliance.

• **Tax Compliance**: International tax laws and treaties impact how wealth is managed and reported. Countries have specific rules for reporting foreign income, investments, and assets. Wealth managers must ensure compliance with these regulations to avoid penalties and optimise tax strategies.

• **Financial Reporting Standards**: Different countries have varying financial reporting standards, which can affect how financial statements and disclosures are prepared and presented. Understanding these standards is crucial for managing international investments and ensuring accurate reporting.

- **Investment Regulations**: Regulations governing investments, such as securities laws and regulations related to financial markets, impact how investments are made and managed. These regulations vary by country and affect cross-border investments and financial transactions.

- **Regulatory Bodies**: Various regulatory bodies oversee financial markets and institutions. For example, the U.S. Securities and Exchange Commission (SEC) regulates securities markets in the United States, while the European Securities and Markets Authority (ESMA) oversees financial markets in the European Union. Wealth managers must navigate these regulatory frameworks to ensure compliance and effective wealth management.

Legal Challenges and Solutions

Migrants and wealth managers often encounter legal challenges related to immigration and international wealth management. Addressing these challenges involves understanding legal requirements and seeking appropriate solutions.

- **Immigration Status Issues**: Migrants may face challenges related to maintaining or changing their immigration status. For example, issues with visa renewals, changes in employment status, or compliance with residency requirements can affect legal status.

  - **Solution**: Consulting with immigration attorneys and staying informed about policy changes can help address these issues. Legal professionals can provide guidance on maintaining status and navigating complex immigration procedures.

- **Taxation and Reporting**: Managing tax obligations across multiple jurisdictions can be complex. Migrants may face challenges related to double taxation, tax reporting, and compliance with international tax laws.

  ○ **Solution**: Engaging with tax advisors who specialise in international taxation can help address these challenges. Tax professionals can provide strategies for minimising tax liabilities, ensuring compliance, and optimising tax reporting.

- **Asset Protection and Estate Planning**: Legal issues related to asset protection and estate planning can arise, particularly when dealing with cross-border assets and inheritance laws.

  ○ **Solution**: Wealth managers and legal advisors can assist in developing strategies for protecting assets and planning estates in accordance with local laws. This may include setting up trusts, creating wills, and understanding inheritance regulations in different countries.

- **Legal Disputes and Litigation**: Migrants and investors may encounter legal disputes related to contracts, investments, or property. Resolving these disputes requires understanding the legal framework and seeking appropriate remedies.

  ○ **Solution**: Seeking legal representation and mediation services can help address disputes and reach resolutions. Legal professionals with expertise in international law can provide guidance on resolving conflicts and navigating legal systems.

- **Compliance with Local Laws**: Ensuring compliance with local laws and regulations in both host and home countries is essential. This includes adhering to financial regulations, business laws, and property laws.

○ **Solution**: Staying informed about local legal requirements and working with local legal and financial experts can help ensure compliance and avoid legal issues.

By addressing these regulatory and legal considerations, migrants and wealth managers can navigate the complexities of international relocation and wealth management more effectively. Understanding immigration policies, financial regulations, and legal challenges is crucial for successful migration and financial planning.

Chapter 7: Emerging Trends in Migration and Wealth Management

Technological Advancements

Technology is transforming both wealth management and migration, introducing new tools and platforms that influence how people manage their finances and move across borders.

● **Digital Platforms and Fintech**: Financial technology (fintech) has revolutionised wealth management through digital platforms that offer enhanced accessibility and convenience. Innovations include:

○ **Robo-Advisors**: Automated investment platforms that provide portfolio management and financial planning based on algorithms and data analysis. They offer cost-effective solutions for investors and can be particularly attractive for international clients seeking efficient investment management.

○ **Blockchain and Cryptocurrencies**: Blockchain technology enables secure and transparent transactions, and cryptocurrencies offer new avenues for investment and wealth transfer. These technologies can facilitate cross-border transactions and offer innovative ways to manage and grow wealth.

○ **Digital Banking and Payments**: Digital banks and payment platforms simplify international transactions and currency exchange. They provide real-time access to funds and streamlined financial services, supporting both personal and business migration needs.

● **Data Analytics and Artificial Intelligence (AI)**: Advanced data analytics and AI are transforming wealth management by providing insights into investment opportunities, risk assessment, and financial planning.

○ **Personalised Financial Services**: AI-driven tools offer personalised financial advice and investment recommendations based on individual preferences and financial goals.

○ **Risk Management**: AI algorithms help assess and mitigate financial risks by analysing market trends, economic indicators, and individual investment portfolios.

● **Remote Work and Digital Nomadism**: Technology enables remote work, allowing individuals to live and work from various locations globally. This trend is influencing migration patterns as more people choose to relocate to countries with favourable living conditions while maintaining their careers.

○ **Coworking Spaces**: The rise of coworking spaces and digital nomad hubs supports remote workers and expatriates, providing flexible work environments and networking opportunities.

Future Migration Patterns

Predictions and trends in migration are shaped by evolving economic conditions, financial markets, and other global factors. Key future migration patterns include:

● **Economic Shifts**: Emerging economies and rapidly growing regions are likely to attract skilled professionals and investors seeking new opportunities. Economic shifts, driven by technological advancements and market developments, will influence where people choose to migrate.

○ **Tech Hubs**: Cities known for their technology sectors, such as Silicon Valley, Bangalore, and Shenzhen, will continue to attract talent and investment.

● **Urbanisation**: Increasing urbanisation will drive migration from rural areas to cities as people seek better economic opportunities, improved infrastructure, and higher living standards.

○ **Megacities**: The growth of megacities and urban centres will continue, with individuals moving to these hubs for career opportunities and lifestyle benefits.

● **Investment Migration**: The trend of migration driven by investment opportunities will likely persist, with individuals seeking residency or citizenship in countries offering favourable financial and business conditions.

○ **Residency-by-Investment Programs**: Programs offering residency or citizenship through financial investments will remain popular among high-net-worth individuals seeking global mobility and financial benefits.

● **Geopolitical Changes**: Political stability, regulatory changes, and international relations will influence migration patterns. Shifts in geopolitical landscapes may lead to new migration trends as individuals and businesses adapt to changing conditions.

Impact of Climate Change

Climate change is increasingly influencing migration patterns and wealth management strategies, with far-reaching effects on both environmental conditions and economic stability.

- **Climate-Induced Migration**: Climate change can drive migration as individuals and communities are forced to relocate due to environmental factors such as rising sea levels, extreme weather events, and resource scarcity.

  - **Environmental Refugees**: Populations in vulnerable areas may migrate to safer regions as they face the impacts of climate change, including flooding, droughts, and hurricanes.

- **Investment in Climate Resilience**: Wealth management strategies are adapting to address the risks associated with climate change. Investors are increasingly focusing on sustainable and climate-resilient investments.

  - **Green Investments**: Investments in renewable energy, sustainable agriculture, and climate adaptation technologies are gaining traction as individuals and businesses seek to mitigate environmental risks.

- **Real Estate and Infrastructure**: The impact of climate change on real estate and infrastructure is a growing concern. Properties in high-risk areas may see decreased value or increased insurance costs, influencing investment decisions and migration.

  - **Climate-Safe Locations**: Investors and migrants may prefer locations less susceptible to climate risks, such as higher elevations or regions with more stable weather patterns.

- **Policy and Regulation**: Governments and financial institutions are increasingly implementing policies and regulations to address climate change and promote sustainability.

  - **Climate Policies**: Regulations related to carbon emissions, environmental protection, and climate adaptation are shaping investment strategies and influencing migration decisions.

By examining these emerging trends, we gain insight into how technological advancements, future migration patterns, and climate change are reshaping wealth management and global mobility. Understanding these trends helps individuals, businesses, and policymakers navigate the evolving landscape of migration and finance effectively.

Chapter 8: Case Studies and Success Stories

Successful Migration Stories

In-depth profiles of individuals and families who have successfully navigated migration through strategic wealth management illustrate how effective planning and decision-making can lead to positive outcomes. These stories offer valuable insights into the practical application of wealth management strategies in the context of migration.

1. The Patel Family: Diversifying Wealth and Expanding Horizons

- **Background**: The Patel family, originally from India, had built significant wealth through a successful technology business. With a desire to expand their global footprint and provide their children with international education opportunities, they decided to migrate to Canada.

- **Strategic Migration**: The Patels chose Canada for its stable economy, high quality of life, and favourable immigration policies for skilled professionals and entrepreneurs. They utilised Canada's Investor Visa program, which required a substantial investment in a business and job creation.

- **Wealth Management Strategies**:

  o **Real Estate Investment**: The family invested in high-growth real estate markets in Toronto and Vancouver, leveraging their capital to secure valuable properties.

  o **Business Expansion**: They established a new tech venture in Canada, focusing on innovation and tapping into the local tech ecosystem.

○ **Education and Integration**: The Patels also invested in high-quality education for their children and engaged with local communities to ensure a smooth integration.

• **Outcome**: The Patels successfully expanded their business operations internationally, diversified their investment portfolio, and enjoyed a high standard of living in Canada. Their children benefited from excellent educational opportunities, and the family integrated well into Canadian society.

2. The Gonzalez Family: Navigating Tax Benefits and Business Growth

• **Background**: The Gonzalez family, from Spain, faced high tax burdens and sought a more favourable tax environment. They chose to migrate to Portugal to benefit from its attractive tax incentives for expatriates and investors.

• **Strategic Migration**: Portugal's Golden Visa program, offering residency through investment in real estate, appealed to the Gonzalezes. They purchased multiple properties in Lisbon and Porto, which also allowed them to benefit from Portugal's Non-Habitual Resident (NHR) tax regime.

• **Wealth Management Strategies**:

○ **Tax Optimization**: By relocating to Portugal, the Gonzalezes took advantage of lower income tax rates and tax exemptions on foreign income under the NHR regime.

○ **Real Estate Investment**: They acquired prime real estate, generating rental income and capital gains as Lisbon's property market grew.

○ **Business Ventures**: The family invested in local businesses, contributing to economic growth and diversifying their wealth.

• **Outcome**: The Gonzalezes achieved significant tax savings, enjoyed a high standard of living in Portugal, and saw substantial returns on their real estate investments. Their strategic migration resulted in both financial and lifestyle benefits.

3. The Kim Family: Leveraging Business Opportunities and Global Networks

• **Background**: The Kim family, originally from South Korea, sought to leverage global business opportunities and expand their network. They decided to migrate to Singapore, a hub for international business and finance.

• **Strategic Migration**: Singapore's reputation as a business-friendly environment, combined with its strong financial markets and strategic location in Asia, made it an ideal destination for the Kims.

• **Wealth Management Strategies**:

○ **Business Expansion**: The Kims established a new investment firm in Singapore, focusing on Southeast Asian markets. They utilised Singapore's favourable business regulations and financial infrastructure.

○ **Networking and Partnerships**: They engaged with local business networks and built partnerships with regional firms, enhancing their business prospects.

○ **Investment Diversification**: The family diversified their investments across various sectors, including technology, real estate, and finance, to capitalise on Singapore's dynamic economy.

• **Outcome**: The Kims successfully expanded their business operations, built valuable networks in Asia, and achieved substantial growth in their investment portfolio. Their strategic migration positioned them well in the global market.

Impactful Migration Events

Historical and contemporary migration events have shaped migration trends and wealth management strategies, offering lessons and insights into the broader dynamics of global mobility.

1. The Gold Rush Migration (19th Century)

• **Event Overview**: The California Gold Rush (1848–1855) led to a massive influx of migrants from around the world seeking wealth and opportunities in the United States. This migration transformed California's economy and demographics.

• **Impact on Migration**: The Gold Rush attracted diverse groups, including Europeans, Latin Americans, and Chinese immigrants, who migrated in search of fortunes. It also led to the rapid growth of cities like San Francisco.

• **Impact on Wealth Management**: The event highlighted the potential for sudden wealth accumulation and the need for financial planning in uncertain environments. It influenced future migration patterns, emphasising the allure of economic opportunities in shaping global movement.

2. Post-War European Migration (1950s-1960s)

• **Event Overview**: After World War II, Europe experienced significant migration as countries sought to rebuild and attract labour for economic growth. Many migrants moved from Southern Europe to Northern and Western Europe for job opportunities.

• **Impact on Migration**: This migration was driven by economic needs and labour shortages in countries like Germany, the UK, and France. It shaped the labour markets and social policies in host countries.

• **Impact on Wealth Management**: The post-war migration emphasised the role of economic opportunities in driving migration and the need for effective integration policies. It also highlighted the importance of remittances and the impact of migration on home country economies.

3. The Rise of Global Cities (21st Century)

● **Event Overview**: In the 21st century, global cities such as New York, London, Hong Kong, and Singapore have become major hubs for finance, technology, and international business. These cities have attracted global talent and investors.

● **Impact on Migration**: The rise of global cities has influenced migration patterns, with professionals and investors relocating to these hubs for career and business opportunities. The cities have become magnets for skilled labor and high-net-worth individuals.

● **Impact on Wealth Management**: The prominence of global cities has driven the growth of financial services and investment opportunities. Wealth management strategies have adapted to address the needs of international clients and navigate the complexities of global markets.

By exploring these successful migration stories and impactful events, this chapter illustrates how strategic wealth management and historical contexts shape migration experiences and outcomes. These case studies and events provide valuable lessons for individuals and families navigating migration and wealth management in an increasingly interconnected world.

Conclusion

Summary of Key Findings

Throughout this book, we have explored the intricate relationship between migration, wealth management, and financial markets. Here is a recap of the key insights:

• **Migration Dynamics**: Historical and modern migration trends reveal that economic opportunities, political stability, and environmental factors drive global movement. Skilled labour migration, economic migration, and refugee movements each play distinct roles in shaping migration patterns.

• **Wealth Management and Migration**: Wealth management strategies significantly impact migration decisions. High-net-worth individuals and families use financial planning, tax optimization, and investment opportunities to facilitate relocation. Case studies of successful migrations demonstrate how strategic wealth management can lead to positive outcomes.

• **Wall Street and Global Migration**: Wall Street's influence on global migration is profound. Fluctuations in financial markets impact migration decisions by affecting economic conditions and investment opportunities. The relocation of financial services professionals and the rise of financial hubs underscore the connection between stock markets and migration trends.

• **Investment Strategies and Migration**: Investment opportunities abroad, such as real estate and business ventures, often drive migration. Tax optimization and wealth preservation strategies also play a critical role in shaping migration decisions. Examples of investment-driven migration highlight the diverse ways in which individuals and families seek financial advantages through relocation.

• **Economic and Social Implications**: Migration has significant effects on both host and home countries. Host countries experience impacts on labour markets and public services, while home countries face challenges related to brain drain and remittances. Global economic trends, influenced by financial markets, further affect migration and wealth management.

- **Regulatory and Legal Considerations**: Immigration policies, financial regulations, and legal challenges shape the migration and wealth management landscape. Navigating these complexities requires understanding immigration laws, financial compliance, and addressing legal issues related to cross-border wealth.

- **Emerging Trends**: Technological advancements, such as fintech and AI, are transforming wealth management and migration. Future migration patterns will be influenced by economic shifts, urbanisation, and climate change. These trends highlight the evolving nature of migration and financial strategies in a rapidly changing world.

Future Outlook

The future of migration and wealth management will be shaped by several factors:

- **Technological Innovations**: The continued evolution of technology will impact how wealth is managed and how migration decisions are made. Advances in digital platforms, blockchain, and AI will offer new tools and opportunities for managing global assets and facilitating international mobility.

- **Economic Conditions**: Financial markets will continue to influence migration patterns. Economic stability, growth prospects, and investment opportunities will drive migration trends, with global cities and emerging economies playing pivotal roles.

- **Climate Change**: As climate change accelerates, it will increasingly affect migration patterns and wealth management strategies. Environmental factors will drive relocation and investment in climate-resilient assets and sustainable practices.

- **Regulatory Changes**: Evolving immigration policies and financial regulations will impact international migration and wealth management. Staying informed about regulatory changes and adapting strategies accordingly will be crucial for navigating future challenges.

Final Thoughts

The interconnectedness of migration, wealth management, and global financial systems is a testament to the complex and dynamic nature of our world. Migration is not just about moving from one place to another; it is a multifaceted process influenced by economic opportunities, financial strategies, and regulatory environments.

Wealth management plays a crucial role in facilitating migration, offering individuals and families the means to optimise their financial situations and navigate new environments. Similarly, financial markets, particularly Wall Street, have a profound impact on migration trends, shaping where and how people move.

As we look to the future, understanding the interplay between these factors will be essential for individuals, businesses, and policymakers. By recognizing the influence of financial markets, embracing technological advancements, and addressing emerging challenges such as climate change, we can better navigate the evolving landscape of migration and wealth management.

The journey of migration is a reflection of broader global trends and personal aspirations. It is an ongoing process of adaptation and opportunity, driven by the quest for a better life, financial stability, and strategic growth.

Rationalising migration and capitalism involves understanding how migration fits within capitalist systems and how capitalism can influence and be influenced by migration patterns. Here are key points to consider:

1. Economic Integration

Labour Markets: Migration helps address labour shortages in various sectors. Capitalist economies often require flexible labour markets to thrive, and migration can fill gaps in both high-skill and low-skill jobs.

Economic Growth: Migrants can stimulate economic growth by increasing demand for goods and services, starting businesses, and contributing to innovation. This growth benefits capitalist economies by expanding markets and creating new opportunities.

2. Capital Accumulation

Investment Opportunities: Migrants often bring new ideas and entrepreneurial skills, contributing to the creation of new industries and investment opportunities. This aligns with capitalist goals of capital accumulation and market expansion.

Resource Allocation: Migration can lead to more efficient resource allocation. By moving to areas with higher economic opportunities, migrants can help balance labour supply and demand, improving overall productivity.

3. Global Trade and Capital Flows

Trade Networks: Migration often strengthens global trade networks. Migrants can serve as bridges between their home countries and host countries, facilitating trade and investment.

Capital Mobility: In a capitalist system, capital is expected to move freely. Migration of labour complements this by enabling the movement of human capital to where it is most needed, supporting economic efficiency and growth.

4. Addressing Social and Economic Challenges

Inequality: While capitalism can drive economic growth, it can also lead to inequality. Migration can help address some of these disparities by providing new opportunities for migrants and stimulating economic activity in both origin and destination countries.

Social Integration: Effective integration policies can help migrants contribute positively to capitalist economies, reducing social tensions and maximising their economic contributions.

5. Policy Implications

Regulatory Frameworks: To rationalise migration within capitalism, it's crucial to develop policies that balance economic needs with social considerations. This includes fair labour practices, support for migrant integration, and protection against exploitation.

Economic Incentives: Implementing incentives for businesses to hire and invest in migrant communities can enhance the benefits of migration within capitalist systems.

6. Ethical Considerations

Human Rights: Rationalising migration within capitalism must consider ethical dimensions, such as the rights of migrants and the impact on local communities. Policies should aim to ensure fair treatment and equitable opportunities for all.

Sustainable Development: Integrating migration into capitalist frameworks should support sustainable development goals, ensuring that economic benefits are distributed fairly and contribute to long-term social and environmental well-being.

By understanding these dynamics and developing thoughtful policies, capitalism can harness the benefits of migration while addressing potential challenges. This approach ensures that migration contributes positively to economic growth and social cohesion within capitalist systems.

Don't miss out!

Visit the website below and you can sign up to receive emails whenever Sixolisiwe Dabula publishes a new book. There's no charge and no obligation.

https://books2read.com/r/B-A-KKIZB-KIZAE

BOOKS 2 READ

Connecting independent readers to independent writers.

About the Author

Everyone can be a worker but not everyone can be rich, Why is the economy based on wealth?